The Indigenous Roots of a Mexican-American Family

Donna S. Morales
and
John P. Schmal

HERITAGE BOOKS
2008

HERITAGE BOOKS

AN IMPRINT OF HERITAGE BOOKS, INC.

Books, CDs, and more—Worldwide

For our listing of thousands of titles see our website
at
www.HeritageBooks.com

Published 2008 by
HERITAGE BOOKS, INC.
Publishing Division
100 Railroad Ave. #104
Westminster, Maryland 21157

Copyright © 2003 Donna S. Morales and John P. Schmal

Other Heritage Books by Donna S. Morales and John P. Schmal:

Mexican-American Genealogical Research: Following the Paper Trail to Mexico

The Dominguez Family: A Mexican-American Journey

The Indigenous Roots of a Mexican-American Family

Other Heritage Books by John P. Schmal:

Naturalizations of Mexican Americans: Extracts, Volumes 1-4

The Journey to Latino Political Representation

Other Heritage Books by John P. Schmal and Jennifer Vo:

A Mexican-American Family of California: In the Service of Three Flags

International Standard Book Numbers
Paperbound: 978-0-7884-2469-4
Clothbound: 978-0-7884-7309-8

DEDICATION

We dedicate this work to our parents:

Daniel S. Morales

Bessie Morales

George J. Schmal

Leona C. Schmal

TABLE OF CONTENTS

TABLE OF CONTENTS

TABLE OF CONTENTS

TABLE OF CONTENTS

ILLUSTRATIONS

PREFACE

by Professor José Rósbel López Morín
Chicano Educator

I first came to know of John Schmal in January 2001 soon after the completion of my dissertation at the University of California, Los Angeles. Our first encounter was via Email. A memorandum was sent to UCLA's César Chávez Center announcing a seminar, free of charge, for "Hispanic" genealogical research. The class caught the attention of several faculty, staff, and students because—like most Mexican Americans—our family history is not a chronicle that is recorded, but one that is passed through word of mouth from generation to generation.

It is through oral tradition that our collective memory is kept alive as Mexican Americans. Many of these stories begin somewhere in rural Mexico, in small ranchos with no running water or electricity, and end with an immigration into the United States. The trials and tribulations of our

PREFACE

ancestors serve as a source of inspiration for many of us today given that these stories are at the core of who we are as Mexican Americans.

Unable to attend the seminar, I managed to keep in touch with John via Email and, in time, we investigated my family tree. I discovered that his knowledge of Mexican and Mexican American genealogy and the history of indigenous Mexico is that of a professional, and his enthusiasm for information in the field makes him a specialist.

As a part-time lecturer in the César Chávez Center, Elena Mohseni (the office administrator) and I arranged to have John give a brief presentation in my spring (2001) course entitled, "Representation of the Indigenous People." We felt that Mr. Schmal's expertise would be of value to the students, and Elena and I were correct. The students enjoyed his presentation and some made plans to meet with him to investigate their family history. Their impression of John

PREFACE

was that "although he wasn't born in Mexico, Mexico was born inside of him." This is a tribute to John Schmal's work and dedication.

The reader will appreciate Donna Morales and John Schmal's *The Indigenous Roots of a Mexican American Family* for it is the story of the majority of Mexican Americans. In accessible form, the narrative synthesizes the story of the Mexican people—a history that is multi-dimensional and complex. And throughout the narration, John makes the history relevant to Mexican and Mexican Americans when he allows the reader to learn about Donna Morales's family, whose ancestors migrated from the states of Jalisco and Zacatecas.

To make history personal allows us to understand that in some way or another, we all belong to the Morales family and that Donna's story is an American story and one of all people as well.

ACKNOWLEDGEMENTS

In assembling the information for this book, we have many people and organizations to thank for their contributions, support, or suggestions. These include the following: Bessie Dominguez Morales, the Santa Monica Public Library, the UCLA Young Research Library, the Los Angeles Family History Center, the Kansas City Star, the Simmons Funeral Home, Carole Turner, the National Archives Regional Administration, the Immigration and Naturalization Service, and the Instituto Nacional de Estadística Geografía e Informática (INEGI).

We are grateful to Professor Martha Menchaca for allowing us to utilize a number of quotes from her authoritative work on race in colonial Mexico, *Reconstructing History, Constructing Race: The Indian, Black, and White Roots of Mexican Americans* (published by the University of Texas Press, 2001). We offer many thanks to José Rósbel López Morin for writing our Preface. His support and interest in this story is greatly appreciated.

ACKNOWLEDGEMENTS

We thank the Center for Latin American Studies at Arizona State University for permitting us to utilize many quotations by the late great Philip Wayne Powell, in his masterpiece, *Soldiers, Indians and Silver: North America's First Frontier War*. This work – without a doubt – should be considered the definitive source for information on the indigenous peoples of Zacatecas and Jalisco. This book was very carefully researched and documented and we strongly recommend this reading for anyone who wants to know more about the Chichimeca War of 1550-1590.

We give a special "Thank you" to our illustrator, Eddie Martinez, for the maps that he put together for us. And finally, we are most grateful to Eleanor Clark (the sister of Donna Morales) for the family photographs used in this work.

INTRODUCTION
by Donna S. Morales

Mexican Americans are the face of Native America. I came to that conclusion a few years after having looked in the mirror each morning for so many years. I was born and raised in the heart of America (Kansas), but my grandparents came to the United States during the Mexican Revolution and, as a result I had to look to Mexico to understand what my true identity is.

The Mexican Americans of today have a unique and special legacy. While our past is firmly entrenched in Mexico, our present and our future are inextricably linked to our American identity. Mexican Americans are indeed the face of Native America. We have a special legacy because North America has been our home for thousands of years. All you have to do is look at our faces, our eyes, and our hair and you can see the nomadic hunters who crossed the Bering Strait some 20,000 years ago.

INTRODUCTION

First and foremost, I proudly call myself an American citizen and – specifically – a Mexican American. But my ancestors lived for many years under the Spanish colonial administration in Mexico. And, for this reason, part of my heritage is Hispanic. My name is a Spanish surname and the Christian religion that I practice was introduced into Mexico by Europeans. And for at least three centuries, my Morales ancestors spoke the Spanish language.

But my genetic heritage is an intriguing and fascinating collage of many ethnic groups. When most people think of the indigenous peoples of Mexico, they usually think of the Aztecs, the Mexica, the Maya, or the Zapotecs. But an analysis of Mexico's ethnic indigenous groups tells a much more complex story, for the present-day Republic of Mexico is actually a manifestation of many Indian nations, subdued, absorbed and assimilated under a central Hispanic culture.

INTRODUCTION

"The Indigenous Roots of a Mexican-American Family" is the story of my indigenous roots. Although my ancestors carried the Spanish surname Morales, they were in fact poor Indian laborers in northern Jalisco during the Seventeenth Century. And, in fact, the history of my Morales roots is very typical of the family history of many central and northern Mexican families.

When Mexican Americans decide to explore their roots and find the names of their ancestral towns in Mexico, they are sometimes very pleased. Many of them will say, "At last, I will be able to find out which Indian tribe my ancestors belonged to." However, the search for ethnic identity in Mexico is much more complex.

INTRODUCTION

War, settlements, agriculture, the mining industry, the hacienda system, encomiendas, and slavery have all contributed to major population movements that transformed, displaced and integrated the pre-Hispanic Indian population of Mexico. Because of these factors, many central and northern Mexican communities lost their homogenous character.

In the case of my Morales ancestors from Lagos de Moreno in northern Jalisco, there is no simple answer to the question of "Who Am I?" The Guamares, Caxcanes, Tecuexes, and Guachichile Indians all lived within the vicinity of Lagos de Moreno. The wars that Spaniards fought with and against these indigenous groups during the Sixteenth Century will be discussed at length.

As it turns out, the Spaniards who came to northern Jalisco and southern Zacatecas where my ancestors lived brought Mexica, Tlaxcalans, Cholulans, Otomís and Tarascans with them. These native peoples from other parts of Mexico served the Spaniards well and played an important role in the pacification of the Guamares, Guachichiles, Caxcanes, and Tecuexes. The late historian John Wayne Powell – who has contributed so much to the understanding of early colonial Zacatecas and Jalisco – concludes that with the intermarriage, cultural mixing and assimilation of the Spaniards and Indian groups, "the sixteenth-century land of war thus became fully Mexican in its mixture."

But my original ethnic identity is only part of this story. During the Seventeenth Century, my indigenous ancestors – working for Spanish land owners – became Christian subjects of a European monarch. During this time, all manifestation of our original Indian identity disappeared forever. But the Spanish colonial authorities and parish priests employed racial classifications in their dealings with their Mexican indigenous subjects. As a result, my Morales ancestors remained classified as Indians and – in some cases – as mulatos and mestizos.

INTRODUCTION

As a poor Mexican-Indian family, my Morales and Delgado ancestors labored in the silver mines and agricultural fields surrounding Lagos de Moreno. But, with independence from Spain, my ancestors became classified as the citizens of the Mexican Republic.

However, plagued by the political turmoil of the Nineteenth Century and the vestiges of a racist colonial authority, the lives of my ancestors improved only slightly. The problems that Mexico carried into the Twentieth Century finally came to a head in 1910 with the beginning of the Mexican Revolution.

The Mexican Revolution was a devastating civil war that cost the lives of almost two million Mexicans: in essence, one of every eight Mexican citizens lost his or her life. It was this terrible war that brought my family to the United States. And it was in Kansas City, Kansas that my family settled and flourished for the rest of the century.

INTRODUCTION

Today my family can look back and see that we have evolved over the centuries. From Indian warriors we were converted to Christian Indian laborers. From laborers we evolved into citizens of a new nation, and in Twentieth Century, we became American citizens. This evolution is – as a matter of fact – the same process that almost every other Mexican-American family has experienced. In other words, this is story shared by many.

THE ORIGINS OF MY PEOPLE

Do the Americas have a common history? To the extent that all the Americas, from their earliest settlement to the present day, have had in occupation the people called Indians, the answer is yes. Indians are the link that binds "Latin America" to "Anglo-America." All the Americas are Indian America. Every European invader and colonizer was met by Indians, whether he came from Spain, Portugal, France, England, Sweden, or the Netherlands in the earlier days of Europe's "discovery," or whether he came from Italy or Russia or Germany in the nineteenth century. Whether he was Catholic, Protestant, Jew, Muslim, Buddhist, or Atheist, he came to the land of Indians; and no matter whether he sat down on ocean shores, river valleys, mountains, plains, or deserts, he found Indians there first....[1]

The Face of Native America

My name is Donna Morales and I am a Mexican-American woman. As a Mexican American, I have inherited a special legacy. This legacy was passed down to me from my parents and grandparents and is a source of great pride to me and many other Mexican Americans.

---

[1] Francis Jennings, *The Founders of America* (New York: W. W. Norton & Company, 1993), p. 15.

1

THE ORIGINS OF MY PEOPLE

While the ancestors of many Americans came to the United States fifty, one hundred, or two hundred years ago from England, France, Germany, Africa, Japan, Ireland, China, Syria, Lebanon, Rumania, Norway, Finland, Italy, or Russia, my ancestors have lived on this continent – North America – for many thousands of years.

It is important to understand that the Mexican-American heritage is very multi-dimensional. Although most of us carry Spanish surnames and practice the Christian religion that was given to us by the Spanish missionaries, our genetic heritage tells a different story. Mexican Americans are the face of Native America. When you look at our hair and gaze into our faces, you can see the nomadic hunters who crossed the Bering Strait 20,000 years ago.

Mexican Americans are proud because we know that North America has been our home for thousands of years. Whoever came to the Western Hemisphere after 1492 found us waiting on the shores of North America. And wherever we may live in North America, whether it be Zacatecas,

THE ORIGINS OF MY PEOPLE

Jalisco, Kansas, Texas or California, we know that our ancestors traveled through at one time or another in the last 20,000 years.

Beringia

Originally, there is said to have been a migration of people over what is now called the Bering Strait, which is located between the far eastern coast of Russian Siberia and the western coastline of Alaska. A "bridge" existed in this area because the glaciers locked up so much water that the oceans were more than three hundred feet lower 20,000 years ago than they are today. This drop in sea level exposed a massive unglaciated stretch of land which is now referred to as the *Bering Land Bridge.*

One thousand miles wide from north to south, this natural bridge stretched from Siberia to Alaska and was more like a subcontinent. Even at the height of the ice age, the glaciers were spotty in this area. So this subcontinent – which some archaeologists now call *Beringia* – was full of marshes and bayous and represented an ice-free corridor between glacier complexes. It was thus possible that human travelers were able to travel through this area down the east side of the Canadian Rockies towards the interior of the North American continent.[2]

Migrations

There is a great deal of controversy about the timing of the Beringia crossings. Most archaeologists believe that the first migrants crossed Beringia sometime between 10,000 and 30,000 years ago, moving across in two or more migration waves over a long period of time, ending when the seas rose to drown the land bridge.

Dr. Scott Elias of the University of Colorado's Institute of Arctic and Alpine Research, utilizing radiocarbon dating of fossils from the youngest terrestrial sediments found on the Bering and Chukchi Sea shelves, has estimated that the link between the two continents was probably flooded around

---

[2] *Ibid.*, pp. 26-27.

THE ORIGINS OF MY PEOPLE

10,500 B.P.[3] When the level of the Pacific Ocean had risen to within 100 feet of its present level, water spilled across Beringia into the Arctic Ocean and cut the Americas off from Eurasia.

These early migrations consisted of small bands of hunters who were simply following their prey across the landscape. As these Arctic travelers slowly trekked eastward, little did they realize that many of their descendants would live in both tropical and arid climates. On the following page is a map of North America that illustrates the extent of Beringia and the possible migration routes of the early Indians.[4] It is likely that the early migrants may have traveled along the western and eastern flanks of the Rocky Mountains into what we now call the contiguous fifty states.

---

[3] Email correspondence of Dr. Scott Elias, November 9, 2002. Dr. Elias' research employed cores that had been previously collected by the U.S. Geological Survey.

[4] Illustration by Eddie Martinez.

THE ORIGINS OF MY PEOPLE

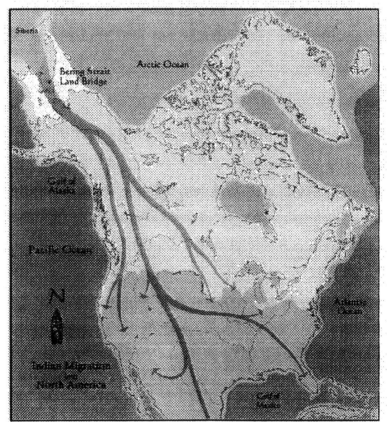

The Native American Migrations

THE ORIGINS OF MY PEOPLE

The primal American people adapted locally and diversely to an extraordinary variety of climatic and topographical conditions in the Americas. Traveling through and living in northern regions in which edible plants were probably scarce and of short seasonal duration, these people eventually developed the tools and weapons required of hunters, gatherers, and fishers.

In this respect, they became experts, searching out mastodons, woolly mammoths, caribou, bison, reindeer, and smaller prey. As time progressed and various groups moved south or along the coastal routes, many of these "Asians" found nourishment by catching fish, shellfish, aquatic mammals, and birds.[5]

Over time, however, these first Americans would find themselves subject to what the late historian Francis Jennings had called the "iron law of population size: in proportion as human numbers increase, the adequacy of wild food resources diminishes. Land enough for ten people is

---

[5] Francis Jennings, *op. cit.*, pp. 31-32.

not enough for twenty."[6]   In short, as the population of a locality increased, the resources of the habitat were stretched to the limit. The natives came into competition with one another and with their prey, gathering the wild plants that were also needed to nourish their game.

At this point, one population group would usually split into two, and the second group would move on "over the next hill" to start what would eventually become a new cultural and linguistic group.

Linguistic Differentiation

As a result of this gradual cultural diffusion, thousands of Indian societies would evolve from the original Asian stock, each having its own language, culture, and territory. A great movement of the primeval travelers took place southward along the eastern slopes of the Sierra Nevada Mountains through the Great Basin of the United States, and thence through Mexico, Central America, and South America.

---

[6] *Ibid.*, p. 41.

THE ORIGINS OF MY PEOPLE

The author Linda Newton believes that the first travelers reached South America as early as 20,000 B.P. (Before the Present) and has estimated that they reached the tip of Tierra del Fuego in South America between 9,000 B.P. and 7,000 B.P.[7] One impressive archaeological site – Monte Verde – located in south central Chile a few miles from the Pacific Ocean, is believed to be 13,000 years old. By about 12,000 years ago, it is believed that the Indians had spread to all the unglaciated sections of both American continents.[8]

It would be impossible to determine exactly how many Indian societies came and went over the last 10,000 years. However, most anthropologists and linguists agree that when *Cristóbal Colón* (Christopher Columbus) first stepped foot in the Americas in 1492, the Native American tribes in the Western Hemisphere may have spoken as many as 2,000 different languages and dialects.

---

[7] Linda Newton, "Pre-Columbian Settlement," *Cambridge Encyclopedia of Latin America and the Caribbean* (New York: Cambridge University Press, 1985), 1: pp. 128-133; Matt S. Meier and Feliciano Ribera, *Mexican Americans, American Mexicans: From Conquistadors to Chicanos* (New York: Hill and Wang, 1993), p. 10.

[8] Carlos M. Jiménez, *The Mexican American Heritage* (Berkeley: TQS Publications, 1994), pp. 26-35.

THE ORIGINS OF MY PEOPLE

The linguistics experts, Victor Golla and Terrence Kaufman, in their recent studies of genetic linguistics, believe that the original number of languages and language families in the Western Hemisphere at the time of contact was 1,000. Of this total, the authors believe that 325 languages families were spoken in North America, 125 in Middle America, and 550 in South America.[9]

Doctors Kaufman and Golla, however, believe that by 1950, only 600 of these languages were still surviving, with 200 in North America, 100 in Middle America, and 300 in South America. These New World languages can be further divided into eighty established language families and 83 classificatory language isolates.[10]

With these statistics in mind, we can thus envision that the original hunters and gatherers who made their way across

---

[9] Terrence Kaufman and Victor Golla, "Language Groupings in the New World: Their Reliability and Usability in Cross-Disciplinary Studies," in Colin Renfrew (ed.), *America Past, America Present: Genes and Languages in the Americas and Beyond* (Cambridge: The McDonald Institute for Archaeological Research, 2000), p. 48.

[10] *Ibid.*

THE ORIGINS OF MY PEOPLE

Beringia thousands of years ago became the ancestors of a very large and diverse group of people. Over the centuries, hundreds of ethnic groups – speaking a multitude of languages and dialects – have gradually evolved from the original stock.

CULTURAL DIFFUSION IN MEXICO

The ancient people who came to Mexico did not find broad connecting valleys, river systems like the Hwang Ho or the Mississippi, where people as well as streams could flow together, mingle, and become one. The "empires" which the Indians built before the coming of the Spaniards hung together loosely; the great Maya, Zapotec, Toltec-Aztec, Mixtec, and Tarascan civilizations set up hierarchies for tribute payment and created wider circles for trade, but seem barely to have spread religious beliefs and language beyond the bounds of the language group among who they originated...

When the Spaniards came they wrought a slow miracle. They began a remarkable welding together of the diverse Middle American peoples. They did this ...by the dint of hard-working and inspired missionaries, by means of the whipping post and the uprooting of thousands for forced labor... [1]

Agriculture

As the Ice Age gave way to a postglacial warming trend, the early Indians of North America learned to adapt to the climatic changes taking place. The Archaic Period, lasting from about 6,000 to 1,000 B.C., was characterized by a foraging way of life for most of the Indian tribes who

---

[1] Edward H. Spicer, "Ways of Life" in Russell C. Ewing et al., *Six Faces of Mexico* (The University of Arizona Press, 1966), p. 65.

survived by hunting and trapping small game, fishing, or gathering edible wild plants.[2]

However, while many of the Indian tribes continued to live a migratory existence during this period, some innovative natives in central Mexico started to wonder how a permanent and uninterrupted supply of their most important wild plant foods could be obtained and maintained.

Somehow, the nomadic Indians in the valley of Tehuacán in south-central Mexico learned that placing the seed of *teosinte* – the grass-like ancestor of maize (corn) – in the moist soil would sprout and produce a nourishing vegetable. As soon as an Indian planted a seed in the ground, with the expectation of harvesting an edible fruit or vegetable, he became tied to the land.[3]

Archaeologists have found traces of agriculture in Mexico dating back as early as 7000 B.C. By 3400 B.C., the

---

[2] Carl Waldman, *op. cit.*, p. 5.

[3] Carlos M. Jiménez, *op. cit.*, p. 31.

CULTURAL DIFFUSION IN MEXICO

Mesoamerican Indians were cultivating pumpkins, beans, chili peppers, avocados, potatoes, and tobacco. With a steady and surplus food supply available, a social revolution took place in these Indian societies. Many Mexican Indian tribes started to build their first permanent dwellings, erected temples to honor their gods, and began to watch the movements of heavenly bodies. "Thus it came to be," writes the historian Carlos M. Jiménez, "that, in time, a flowering of the arts and sciences took place and produced the Classical Era of Indian Mexico."[4]

The Diversity of Mexico

The Republic of Mexico, consisting of 756,066 square miles,[5] has a great variety of landscapes and climates. While mountains and plateaus cover more than two-thirds of her landmass, the rest of Mexico's environment is made up of deserts, tropical forests, and fertile valleys. Mexico's many mountain ranges tend to split the country into countless smaller valleys, each forming a world of its own.

---

[4] *Ibid.*, p. 31; Francis Jennings, *op. cit.*, pp. 40-41.

[5] Funk & Wagnalls Corporation, *The World Almanac and Book of Facts, 1995* (Mahwah, New Jersey: Funk & Wagnalls Corporation, 1994), p. 800.

CULTURAL DIFFUSION IN MEXICO

Mexico's "fragmentation into countless mountain valleys, each with its own mini-ecology," according to historian Nigel Davies, led each geographical unit to develop its own language.[6]

This widespread cultural and linguistic diffusion is a key to understanding Mexican history. The remarkable diversity that resulted from this diffusion – in large part – led to Mexico's conquest by the Spaniards. Speaking more than 180 mutually alien languages when the Europeans first arrived, the original Mexican Indians viewed each other with great suspicion from the earliest times.[7] When Hernán Cortés (1485-1547) came to Mexico in 1519, he found a large but fragmented collection of tribes. It was this dissension and lack of cohesion that he exploited to his advantage.

---

[6] Nigel Davies, *The Ancient Kingdoms of Mexico* (London: Penguin Books, 1990), p. 15.

[7] J. Alden Mason, "The Native Languages of Middle America," in *The Maya and Their Neighbors* (New York: D. Appleton-Century Company, 1940), p. 58

CULTURAL DIFFUSION IN MEXICO

In the centuries since then, the language of each Mexican town or community has evolved independently, sometimes becoming less and less intelligible to its neighbors.[8] Thus, almost five centuries after the Conquest, the people of present-day Mexico speak more than 270 indigenous languages and dialects.[9] On the following page, our illustrator Eddie Martinez has created a map to indicate the locations of some of Mexico's most influential pre-Hispanic indigenous groups.

The Olmecs

The first monumental civilization to rise in Mexico was that of a mysterious people called the Olmecs. Living along the Gulf of Mexico coast, the Olmecs flourished in western Tabasco and southern Veracruz. Starting in 1500 B.C., they constructed earthen mounds and stone pyramids. Their

---

[8] Email Communication of Pam Echerd (SIL Information), November 11, 2002.

[9] Source: "Languages of Mexico" Online: http://www.ethnologue.com/show_country.asp?name=Mexico (November 10, 2002) from Barbara F. Grimes (ed), "Ethnologue: Languages of the World" (14th edition), Dallas, Texas: SIL International, 2001.

CULTURAL DIFFUSION IN MEXICO

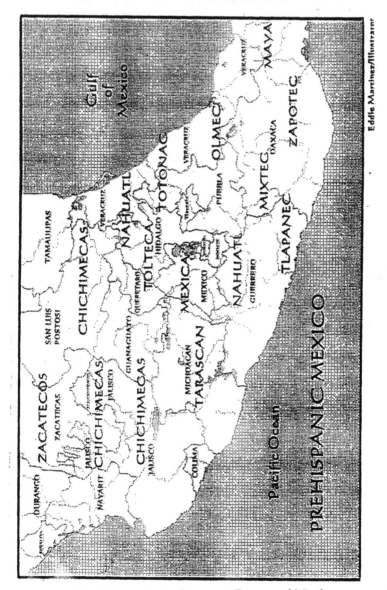

Pre-Hispanic Indigenous Groups of Mexico

civilization, which lasted a thousand years, probably peaked about 800 B.C.

Very little is known about the Olmecs, but it is believed that their decline may have been the result of multiple factors: drought, disease, and invasion from hostile neighboring tribes. However, the archaeologist and educator Richard E.W. Adams has explained that "Olmec culture did not die out, but simply was absorbed and passed on in more or less transformed variations."[10]

The Zapotecs and Mayas

Somewhat later, the Zapotec culture developed high in the Oaxaca Mountains at Monte Albán. They built magnificent temples and developed their own calendar. By A.D. 900, the Zapotec nation was in decline and Monte Albán was abandoned.

The Zapotecs gradually came under the influence of the neighboring Mixtecs who, through warfare and strategic

---

[10] Richard E.W. Adams, *Prehistoric Mesoamerica* (Boston: Little, Brown and Company, 1977), p. 94.

marriages, were able to establish a federation of city-states. The ancient cultures of the Zapotec and Mixtec Indians live on today among many of the Indians of the modern state of Oaxaca.

As a matter of fact, even today, no other state in the Mexican Republic exhibits the level of diversity seen within the modern state of Oaxaca. At present, sixteen different indigenous groups, speaking at least ninety languages and dialects, are recognized within the boundaries of Oaxaca. According to Mexico's National Institute of Statistics, Geography and Informatics (INEGI), 1,027,847 Oaxacan inhabitants over the age of five speak indigenous languages, representing 36.6% of the total population of the state in 1995. As a result, Oaxaca contains 18.7% of the national total of Indian language speakers in Mexico.[11]

To the south and east of the Zapotec nation, in what are now the Mexican states of Yucatán and Chiapas, the Mayan

---

[11] Instituto Nacional de Estadística Geografía e Informática (hereinafter referred to as INEGI), "Social and Demographic Statistics," Online: http://www.inegi.gob.mx/difusion/ingles/fiest.html. November 11, 2002.

CULTURAL DIFFUSION IN MEXICO

Indians developed a remarkable culture that is believed to have flourished from about A.D. 300 to A.D. 900. The Mayan Indians recorded their history and built majestic cities, temples and pyramids. They also developed a practical use for the zero, an idea essential to any higher forms of mathematics. The zero would not be widely used in Europe until 1202 when the Arabs introduced it from India.[12]

The Maya devised a calendar that is considered more accurate than the one we use today. Archaeological studies have also revealed that the Maya were adept at surgery. Sometime between 600 and 700 A.D., most of the classic Mayan cities fell into decay and were abandoned by their inhabitants. The cause of the Mayan decline remains shrouded in mystery to this day.

The Valley of Mexico

The central Mexican Valley, or Anáhuac Valley, sits 8,000 feet above sea level and is surrounded by a ring of mountains and volcanoes. By definition, the Valley of Mexico is not

---

[12] James D. Cockcroft, *Mexico: Class Formation, Capital Accumulation, and the State* (New York: Monthly Review Press, 1983), p. 12.

really a valley, but an internally drained basin situated in the highlands of Mexico's central plateau.

Measuring some 60 miles from north to south, and 40 miles from east to west, the valley covered a fertile area of about 2,500 square miles in Sixteenth Century. The dominance of this central valley is the hallmark of Mexico's Post-Classic Period, which lasted from about A.D. 900 until the Spanish conquest of the Sixteenth Century.[13]

An important cultural center of the central Mexican Valley was Teotihuacán (*The Place of the Gods*). As early as 200 B.C., the inhabitants of Teotihuacán began to emerge as a superior culture in the central valley. The city, situated on the eastern fringe of the Valley, was conceived in a grid pattern and laid out on a colossal scale.

The main thoroughfare, called the Avenue of the Dead, was 150 feet wide and stretched over two miles through the heart

---

[13] Nigel Davies, *The Aztecs: A History* (Norman, Oklahoma: University of Oklahoma Press, 1973), p. 20.

of the ceremonial center. The most striking monument in Teotihuacán is the Pyramid of the Sun. Measuring more than 700 feet at the base, the pyramid rises almost 215 feet high.[14] It is believed that the city of Teotihuacán eventually attained a population of 60,000 to 80,000 inhabitants.[15] Saburo Sugiyama of the Arizona State University writes that Teotihuacán was the "sixth largest city in the world during its period of greatest prosperity."[16]

Teotihuacán, for many centuries, acted as a buffer between the civilized Mexico of the south and the more primitive nomadic people who inhabited the northern regions (now represented by the modern states of Jalisco, Zacatecas, Nayarit, Durango, and Guanajuato). However, the Valley of Anáhuac, writes historian Michael C. Meyer, "was a

---

[14] Michael C. Meyer and William L. Sherman, *The Course of Mexican History* (New York: Oxford University Press, 1987), pp. 20-23.

[15] René Millon, "Teotihuacán: City, State and Civilization," in *Archaeology*, edited by Jeremy A. Sabloff and with the assistance of Patricia A. Andrews, *Supplement to the Handbook of Middle American Indians, vol.1*, (Austin, Texas: University of Texas Press, 1981), p. 221.

[16] Saburo Sugiyama, "Archaeology of Teotihuacan, Mexico," Online: http://archaeology.la.asu.edu/teo/intro/intrteo.htm. August 20, 2001. Copyright 1996, Project Temple of Quetzalcoatl, Instituto Nacional de Antropología e Historia, Mexico/ Arizona State University Department of Anthropology.

compelling lure to rootless peoples seeking a more abundant life. With its equable climate and system of interconnecting lakes bordered by forests full of wild game, it was especially attractive to the nomads of the arid north. Because of its central location the Valley had been, from ancient times, a corridor through which tribes of diverse cultures passed – and sometimes remained."[17]

The Toltecs

When Teotihuacán fell in A.D. 750, the northern tribes, known by the generic term *Chichimecs* ("People of Dog Lineage"), breached the northern frontier. The most significant of these were the Tolteca-Chichimeca, or Toltecs, who were believed to have originated in southern Zacatecas.[18]

From approximately A.D. 900 to A.D. 1100, the Toltecs became the dominant Mexican Indians in the Valley of Mexico. The Toltecs conquered and incorporated many

---

[17] Meyer and Sherman, *op. cit.*, p. 53.

[18] *Ibid.*, pp. 36-37.

other Indian tribes of central Mexico and extended their influence to as far south as Oaxaca. The Toltecs, however, treated their subject peoples with cruelty and arrogance, which may have played a role in their eventual demise.

The Mexica

The Mexica Indians are probably the most well known of all Mexico's ancient cultures. This indigenous group had very obscure and humble roots that made their rise to power during the Fifteenth and Sixteenth Centuries even more remarkable.

The Mexica (pronounced "me-shee-ka") Indians represent the most dominant ethnic group within the larger cultural group that we refer to as the Aztecs. All of the Aztec peoples spoke the Náhuatl language, which – in 2000 – was still spoken by 1,448,936 Mexicans. As such the total population of Náhuatl speakers in the present day represents 24 percent of the total indigenous-speaking population of Mexico (6,044,547).[19]

---

[19] INEGI, *Estados Unidos Mexicanos. XII Censo General, 2000.*

Legend tells us that in A.D. 1111, the Mexica Indians left their home in *Aztlán* (The Place of Herons), believed to be located in northwestern Mexico. It is important to note, however, that the Aztlan migrations were not one simple movement of a single group of people.

Instead, as the anthropologist Professor Michael E. Smith of the University of New York, has noted, "when all of the native histories are compared, no fewer than seventeen ethnic groups are listed among the original tribes migrating from Aztlán..." Professor Smith also writes that "the north to south movement of the Aztlan groups is supported by research in historical linguistics."[20]

"The Náhuatl language," explains Professor Smith, is "classified in the Nahuan group of the Uto-Aztecan family of languages." As such, the language of the Aztecs is

---

[20] Michael E. Smith, *The Aztecs* (Cambridge, Massachusetts: Blackwell Publishers, Inc., 1996), pp. 39, 41.

"unrelated to most Mesoamerican language families" and "was a relatively recent intrusion into Mesoamerica."[21]

It is believed that the migrations southward probably took place over several generations. "Led by priests," continues Professor Smith, "the migrants... stopped periodically to build houses and temples, to gather and cultivate food, and to carry out rituals."[22]

After wandering for many years, the various groups eventually arrived in the Valley of Mexico and in neighboring areas. The Mexica were the last to arrive, perhaps around A.D. 1250. Because all of the good land was already occupied, the Mexica were forced to settle in what Professor Smith calls "an undesirable, desolate area of the Valley of Mexico called Chapultepec, 'grasshopper hill' or 'place of the grasshopper.'"[23]

---

[21] *Ibid.*, p. 41.

[22] *Ibid.*, p. 39.

[23] *Ibid.*, p. 40.

CULTURAL DIFFUSION IN MEXICO

In A.D. 1327, the Aztecs established a new home for themselves in the middle of Lake Texcoco, where they founded their capital city of Tenochtitlán. Fifteen years after the founding of Tenochtitlán, the Aztecs achieved dominance in the Valley by forming a triple alliance with their neighbors at Texcoco and Tlacopan.

The Aztec Empire

By the end of the Fifteenth Century, the Mexica had established an elaborate and wide-ranging empire that extended to the Mexican states of Guerrero and Colima. This empire consisted of a diverse population that is believed to have numbered between 10 and 25 million people. The population of Tenochtitlán is believed to have reached 300,000, making it larger than Madrid or Rome.[24] Probably only four cities in Europe – Paris, Venice, Milan, and Naples – had a greater population at this time.

---

[24] Henry F. Dobyns, "Estimating Aboriginal American Population, *Current Anthropology* 7 (1966), pp. 395-449; James D. Cockcroft, *op. cit.*, pp. 7, 320.

CULTURAL DIFFUSION IN MEXICO

With each conquest, the Aztec domain had become more and more ethnically diverse, eventually controlling thirty-eight provinces. But the most important component of this massive empire was the tribute that the Mexica demanded from the various city-states and subject chieftains. This tribute took many forms, including textiles, warriors' costumes, foodstuffs, maize, beans, chilies, cacao, bee honey, salt and human beings (for sacrificial rituals).

The constant demand for tribute goods transformed the Aztec Empire. "When one considers that imperial tribute pouring into the capital two to four times a year together with trade goods imported by Aztec merchants, the volume of incoming wealth was immense."[25] However, this policy – so greedy and hateful to the subject peoples – laid the foundation for the eventual destruction of Tenochtitlán.

---

[25] Michael E. Smith, *op. cit.*, p. 185.

THE CONQUEST OF MEXICO

Hernán Cortés and his small cadre of soldiers encountered the large Totonac center of Cempoallan in east central Mexico. They found... a realm of conquered and dissatisfied Aztec subjects who, ultimately, were rather easily convinced to rebel against their demanding overlords.[1]

Brilliant as it was in certain respects, Aztec civilization thrived on militarism; therefore the character of its fall was consistent with its rise.[2]

An Empire on the Brink

Ruling over an area of about 80,000 square miles of territory extending from the Gulf of Mexico to the Pacific Ocean, and southward to Oaxaca, the Aztec Empire controlled the destinies of at least 15 million people living in thirty-eight provinces. The map on the following page, reproduced from T.R. Fehrenbach's *Fire and Blood: A History of Mexico,*[3] indicates the extent of the Mexican domain.

---

[1] Michael E. Smith and Frances F. Berdan, "Introduction" in Frances F. Berdan et al., *Aztec Imperial Strategies* (Washington, D.C.: Dumbarton Oaks Research Library and Collection, 1996), p. 1.

[2] Meyer and Sherman, *op. cit.,* p. 129.

[3] T.R. Fehrenbach, *Fire and Blood: A History of Mexico* (New York: Macmillan Publishing Co., Inc. 1973).

THE CONQUEST OF MEXICO

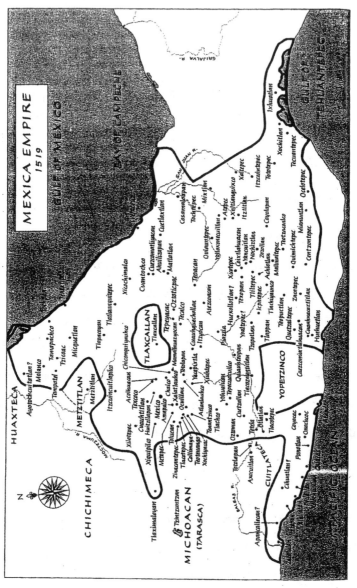

The Mexica Empire in 1519

THE CONQUEST OF MEXICO

In all, the Mexica Emperor Moctezuma II received the tribute of 489 communities. But, for all its wealth and military might, the Aztec Empire lacked the spiritual cohesion that would hold it together during a critical juncture.

Professor Smith observes that "rebellions were a common occurrence in the Aztec empire because of the indirect nature of imperial rule. Local dynasties were left in place as long as they cooperated with the Triple Alliance and paid their tribute" However, a rebellion would take place when "a provincial king would decide that he was strong enough to withhold tribute payments from the empire." In this case, the Triple Alliance would respond by dispatching an army to threaten the errant king and, if necessary, reconquer the city-state." [4]

Professor Smith also observed the existence of "major unconquered enemy states surrounded by imperial territory." The fact that these enclaves remained free of Aztec

---

[4] Michael E. Smith, *The Aztecs*, pp. 55-56.

dominance is some indication that these "enemy states" may have been recognized as "serious and powerful adversaries."[5]

The most powerful enclave, Tlaxcalla, located to the east of the Valley of Mexico, was a confederation of four republics. Tlaxcalla, writes Professor Smith, "was a Nahuatl-speaking area whose population shared a common cultural and ethnic heritage with the rest of the peoples of central Mexico."[6]

Surviving as an independent enclave surrounded by the Aztec Confederation, the Tlaxcalans felt a great enmity toward their Nahua brethren. This hatred would become an important factor after the arrival of the Spaniards in 1519. On the following page, our illustrator Eddie Martinez provides us with the names and locations of many central Mexican indigenous groups at the time of contact.

---

[5] Michael E. Smith, "The Strategic Provinces," in *Aztec Imperial Strategies*, pp. 137-138.

[6] *Ibid.*, p. 140.

THE CONQUEST OF MEXICO

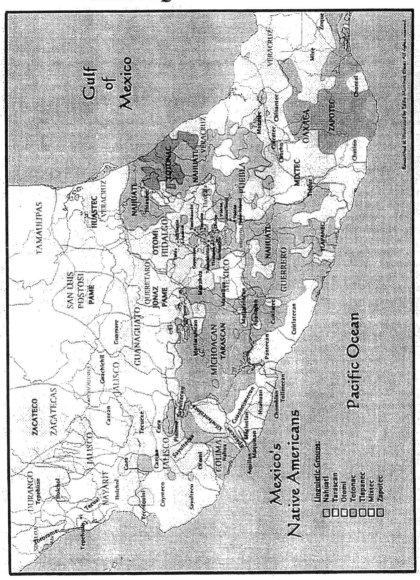

Major Indigenous Groups of Mexico

THE CONQUEST OF MEXICO

Hernán Cortés.

On April 22, 1519, the Spanish adventurer Hernán Cortés landed on the east coast of Mexico not far from the present-day city of Veracruz. In command of 11 ships, 508 men, 16 horses, and a few light cannon, Cortés had been traveling along the Gulf Coast trying to learn about the mineral wealth of this great land mass now called North America.

As the Spaniards disembarked to set up camp on the dunes beyond the beach, they received a friendly reception from the native Totonac Indians, who inhabited this area. The Totonacs inhabited the coastal city-state of Cempoala (Cempoallan), an outlying province of the Aztec Empire, containing some fifty towns.

The town of Cempoala itself contained some 14,000 inhabitants. After receiving a warm reception from the townspeople, Cortés met with Cacique Tlacochcalcatl, the leader of the Totonacs, who explained that the Totonacs were forced to send hundreds of children to the altars of Tenochtitlán for sacrifice each year. For this tribute, the hatred of the Totonacs for the Mexica ran deep.

THE CONQUEST OF MEXICO

Through the Totonacs and other Mexica subjects, Cortés came to understand the complex relationship between the Aztec masters and their subject tribes. Human sacrifice played an integral role in the culture of the Aztecs. However, the author Richard Lee Marks writes, "the Aztecs never sacrificed their own." In their search for sacrificial victims to pacify their gods, the Aztecs extracted men and women from their subject tribes as tribute.[7]

The Tlaxcalans

Eventually, Cortés, supplied with a fresh force of Spanish soldiers and Totonac warriors, made his way into the interior of the continent. When the alien army arrived in the Tlaxcalan Republic, they met with fierce resistance. After several pitched battles, however, both sides found a new respect for one another and agreed to become allies. The Tlaxcalans and Spaniards saw in each other the potential for a great alliance against the military might of the Mexica.

---

[7] Richard Lee Marks, *Cortés: The Great Adventurer and the Fate of Aztec Mexico* (New York: Alfred A Knopf, 1994), p. 200.

THE CONQUEST OF MEXICO

Tlaxcala was a small, densely populated province with a population of 150,000 in 1519. Tlaxcala was actually a "confederation of four republics," ruling over some 200 settlements. Surrounded on all sides and blockaded by the Aztecs, the Tlaxcalan Indians had been subjected to almost continuous warfare and human sacrifice for many decades.

Because of their economic isolation, the Tlaxcalans had no cotton with which to make their clothes. Neither did they have any salt, feathers, or precious stones. This state of perpetual war was very hateful to the Tlaxcalans and by the time that Cortés arrived in Tlaxcala, the confederation represented fertile grounds for an anti-Mexica alliance.

In September, Cortés and his army were invited to stay in Tlaxcala at the invitation of the Tlaxcalan monarch, Xicotenga. During this time, the Tlaxcalans would become the most loyal native allies of the Spaniards as they traveled toward Tenochtitlán. Their allegiance with the Europeans would become an enduring partnership, lasting several centuries.

THE CONQUEST OF MEXICO

Tenochtitlán

By the time Cortés arrived in Moctezuma's capital on November 8, 1519, he was accompanied by an army of at least 6,000 Tlaxcalan and Totonac allies. In the political maneuvering that followed, Cortés, a master of manipulation, was able to capture Moctezuma right in front of his own subjects.

The Spaniards held the Mexica monarch hostage for months. However, in April 1520, Cortés was forced to leave Tenochtitlán for the Gulf Coast to deal with a Spanish political problem. In his absence, he left his friend and lieutenant Pedro de Alvarado in charge of 266 Spanish soldiers and the Tlaxcalans.

While on the Gulf Coast, Cortés reinforced his army from the ranks of newly arrived Spanish forces. With 1,300 Spanish soldiers, thousands of Indian auxiliaries, and new supplies of horses, arms, and gunpowder, the army of Cortés returned to a Tenochtitlán that had changed perceptively.

THE CONQUEST OF MEXICO

In Cortés' absence, Pedro de Alvarado had surrounded and attacked an Aztec religious festival, massacring hundreds of Mexica nobles. At this point, the Mexica inhabitants turned from uneasy hosts to fierce enemies. Under constant and furious assault by the Aztecs, Cortés ordered a strategic retreat from the capital. This event, which took place in the early morning hours of July 1, 1520, has come to be known as *La Noche Triste* (The Night of Sadness).

By the end of the battle, 860 Spaniards, 4,000 Tlaxcalans, and sixty horses were lost. Even with the many reinforcements that Cortés had brought from the coast, this disaster left him with only 420 men. Only twenty-four of the 95 horses survived the exodus. All the survivors – including Cortés – were wounded, and very few firearms or ammunition were left.

As the battered army approached Tlaxcala, they were greeted by their Indian allies and given refuge. "Reviewing their narrow escape," writes Michael C. Meyer, "many of the Spanish veterans wanted nothing more to do with the Aztecs. It required all of Cortés's force of personality and subtle blandishments to prevent mass defections and rebellion among his men. Cortés, who seems never to have wavered in his determination to retake Tenochtitlán, began to lay plans for the return."[8]

It goes without saying that the Spaniards would not have survived their ordeal without the help of their Tlaxcalan allies. The Tlaxcalan chiefs called on Cortés during this dismal time and laid out their conditions for further assistance. The Tlaxcalans requested "perpetual exemption from tribute of any sort, a share of the spoils, and control of two provinces that bordered their land." Cortés agreed to these conditions and, as the author Richard Lee Marks wrote, "Spain substantially kept its promise" to the Tlaxcalans "and exempted them from tribute for the entire period of the Spanish rule in Mexico, nearly three hundred years."[9]

The Spaniards, however, also received more important support from another, unexpected ally. "While the Spaniards

---

[8] Meyer and Sherman, *op. cit.*, p. 124.

[9] Richard Lee Marks, *op. cit.*, p. 188.

rested and recuperated" in Tlaxcala, wrote Richard Lee Marks, "it occurred to Cortés and his men to wonder why the great armies from Tenochtitlán were not pursuing them." The Aztecs had not attacked or laid siege to Tlaxcala, giving the Spaniards and Tlaxcalans precious time to heal and recover from their catastrophic defeat. Later, Cortés would learn that an epidemic of smallpox had devastated Tenochtitlán.[10]

Brought to the shores of Mexico by an African sailor, "the disease had spread with amazing rapidity through the coastal tribes and up into the highland." The disease spread quickly among the Indians, according to Marks, because they "were in the habit of bathing to alleviate almost any ailment that afflicted them. These baths were either communal or the same bathing water was used consecutively by many. But after someone with an open smallpox sore entered the bath, the disease was transmitted to everyone who followed." [11]

---

[10] *Ibid.*, p. 190.

[11] *Ibid.*, pp. 190-191.

The Spaniards, however, never bathed. Although they occasionally washed off the dirt and blood when they had to, "they believed that bathing per se was weakening." And the Tlaxcalans, "always in a state of semi-siege," were not yet exposed to the smallpox.[12]

The Great Coalition

In May 1521, Hernán Cortés, with 900 Spaniards, 118 crossbows and harquebuses, fifteen bronze cannons and three heavy guns, thirteen brigantines, and almost 100,000 Indian warriors, returned to Tenochtitlán to lay siege to the great city. The Aztecs resisted to the last until their people were reduced to eating worms and bark from trees.

On August 13, 1521, after a 75-day siege, Tenochtitlán finally fell. In later years, Aztec historians would state that 240,000 Aztecs died in the siege. While many of the warriors died in battle, others, including most of the women and children, died from starvation and disease.

---

[12] *Ibid.*

THE CONQUEST OF MEXICO

The anthropologist Eric R. Wolf stressed the importance of Cortés' Indian allies in the capture of Tenochtitlán. Wolf writes that "Spanish firepower and cavalry would have been impotent against the Mexica armies without" the support of the Tlaxcalans and the Texcocans. The allies "furnished the bulk of the infantry and manned the canoes that covered the advance of the brigantines across the lagoon of Tenochtitlán." In addition, "they provided, transported, and prepared the food supplies needed to sustain an army in the field. They maintained lines of communication between the coast and highland, and they policed occupied and pacified areas."[13]

Finally, writes Mr. Wolf, the Indian allies also "supplied the raw materials and muscular energy for the construction of the ships that decided the siege of the Mexican capital." In conclusion, he states that while "Spanish military equipment

---

[13] Eric R. Wolf, *Sons of the Shaking Earth* (Chicago: University of Chicago Press, Phoenix Books, 1959), pp. 154-155.

and tactics carried the day," the "Indian assistance determined the outcome of the war."[14]

Nueva España

When Cortés conquered Tenochtitlán in 1521, most of the Aztec Empire of southern Mexico automatically fell under the control of the Spanish Empire. The authors Michael C. Meyer and William L. Sherman discussed this sudden collapse of the mighty Aztec Empire:[15]

> Highly centralized states strongly dependent on a dominant capital are vulnerable, tending to disintegrate quickly when the center falls. Hence the collapse of the imperial capital of Tenochtitlán was tantamount to the surrender of almost all towns under the city's control, and, therefore, much of central Mexico automatically fell to the invaders. There were many other areas of Mexico, however, that had remained outside the Aztec pale. Some threw in with the Spaniards early, and some came around as the Spaniards gained in reputation. But others,

---

[14] *Ibid.*

[15] Meyer and Sherman, *op. cit.*, p. 133.

which had successfully resisted the Aztecs, rejected Spanish overlordship as well.

Throughout the former Aztec Empire and along some of the outlying territories, the Spaniards set up army posts. Spanish priests built churches and began a vigorous campaign to convert the Indians to Roman Catholicism. The newly conquered area was given the name *Nueva España* (New Spain). A series of explorations and conquests would expand Nueva España in all directions during the rest of the century.

The Encomienda System

The conquest of the Aztec Empire was accomplished by Spanish adventurers who had received no pay for their efforts. According to Messrs. Meyer and Sherman, most of them "had gone into debt in order to outfit themselves for the enterprise; all had suffered great hardships and had seen companions die horrible deaths; almost all had been wounded." As the Spanish military began to consolidate its power in Nueva España, the veterans of the Battle of

Tenochtitlàn began to pressure Cortés for some form of reward for their suffering and sacrifice.[16]

Under this pressure, Cortés secured the tribute rolls of the Aztec treasurer, which had paintings that identified the subject towns and the amount of tribute each paid to Tenochtitlán. In all, there were 370 towns, each of which had yielded one-third of its total production to the Aztec Empire.

With this information in hand, Cortés calmed his irate soldiers by distributing to them Indian towns as rewards. This practice, known as *encomienda*, had been used by the Spaniards in the Caribbean with devastating results. The individual receiving the encomienda, known as the *encomendero*, "received the tribute of the Indians, as well as their free labor, in return for which the natives were commended to the encomendero's care. He was to see to

---

[16] *Ibid.*, p. 131.

their conversion to Christianity, to ensure good order in the village, and in all ways to be responsible for their welfare."[17]

The result of the encomienda system, writes Mr. Meyer, was a "system, subjected to every imaginable abuse," that would keep "Indians in a state of serfdom." Under the system, "Indians were overworked, separated from their families, cheated, and physically maltreated. The encomienda was the institution most responsible for demeaning the native race and creating economic and social tragedies that persisted in one guise or another into modern times."[18]

The Decimation of the Indigenous People

Several factors contributed to the dramatic decline of the indigenous people of Mexico. It is believed that the Indian population of the Valley of Mexico declined from 1.5 million in 1521 to 300,000 in 1570. During the same period, the population of all of Mexico, which is believed to have

---

[17] *Ibid.*

[18] *Ibid.*

been 25 million in 1521, dropped to three million inhabitants.

The decline heightened Indian suffering as the encomenderos competed for increasingly scarce labor power. The whip, imprisonment, torture, rape, and killing became standard weapons for enforcing labor discipline. Although the Indians were exempted from taxes and tithes, they were required to pay a yearly head-tax, called tribute. Both men and women were herded into mines and *obrajes* (textile workshops) to labor for long hours.[19]

Although the encomienda caused a great deal of suffering and death, historians believe that disease played the central role in the depopulation of Mexico's native population. The physical isolation of the Indians in the Americas is the primary reason for which disease caused such havoc with the native population. The physical isolation resulted in a biological isolation and a natural quarantine from the rest of

---

[19] James D. Cockcroft, *op. cit.*, p. 20.

the planet and from a wide assortment of communicable diseases. When smallpox first ravaged through Mexico in 1520, no Indian had immunity to the disease.

During the first century of the conquest, the Mexican Indians suffered through 19 major epidemics. They were exposed to smallpox, chicken pox, diphtheria, influenza, scarlet fever, measles, typhoid, mumps, influenza, and cocoliztli (a hemorrhagic disease). Although this devastation made the conquest an easier task, it also caused a labor shortage that would lead to the introduction of African slaves.

This is the story of the conquest of central Mexico. As we shall see in the following chapters, the Spanish conquest of the northern regions – where my ancestors lived – was a much more drawn out conflict that would last decades.

THE CHICHIMECAS

Hernán Cortés, the Conqueror, defeated the Aztecs in a two-year campaign.... [His] stunning success created an illusion of European superiority over the Indian as a warrior. But this lightning-quick subjugation of such massive and complex peoples as the Tlaxcalan, Aztec, and Tarascan, proved to be but prelude to a far longer military struggle against the peculiar and terrifying prowess of Indian America's more primitive warriors.[1]

It took the Spaniards and their Indian allies a full fifty years to achieve general pacification of the Chichimeca tribes of the sixteenth-century silver frontier....[2]

Center-West Mexico

From the earliest of times, my indigenous ancestors lived in what the historian Eric Van Young of the University of California at San Diego has called "the Center-West Region" of Mexico.[3] This cultural region, according to Dr. Van Young, includes all of the modern states of Jalisco,

---

[1] Philip Wayne Powell, *Soldiers, Indians and Silver; North America's First Frontier War* (Tempe, Arizona: Center for Latin American Studies, Arizona State University, 1975), p. vii.

[2] *Ibid.*, p. 31.

[3] Eric Van Young, "The Indigenous Peoples of Western Mexico from the Spanish Invasion to the Present," in Richard E.W. Adams and Murdo J. MacLeod (ed.), *The Cambridge History of the Native Peoples of the Americas, Volume II: Mesoamerica, Part 2* (Cambridge, U.K.: Cambridge University Press, 2000), pp. 136-186.

THE CHICHIMECAS

Michoacán, Colima, Nayarit, and Aguascalientes, as well as parts of Zacatecas and Guanajuato, amounting to about one-tenth of Mexico's national territory.

In the case of my ancestors, we are most interested in the indigenous groups that occupied northern Jalisco, Aguascalientes, and southern Zacatecas. My earliest recorded Morales ancestors lived in the northern Jalisco towns of Lagos de Moreno and Ciénega de Mata, which lay in close proximity to the states of Zacatecas, Aguascalientes, San Luis Potosí, and Guanajuato.

The modern state of Jalisco consists of 31,152 square miles (80,684 square kilometers) located in the west central portion of the Mexican Republic. But the state of Jalisco did not exist as a political entity in the Sixteenth Century. Most of colonial Jalisco was, in fact, part of the Spanish province of Nueva Galicia, which embraced some 180,000 kilometers ranging from the Pacific Ocean to the foothills of the Sierra Madre Occidental. Besides the present-day state of Jalisco, Nueva Galicia also included the states of Aguascalientes, Zacatecas, Nayarit, and the part of San Luis Potosí.

THE CHICHIMECAS

Across this broad range of territory, a wide array of indigenous groups lived before 1522 (the year of contact with Spanish explorers). Domingo Lázaro de Arregui, in his *Descripción de la Nueva Galicia* – published in 1621 – wrote that 72 languages were spoken in the Spanish colonial province of Nueva Galicia. In order to convey to the reader an idea of the remarkable diversity of Center-West Mexico's pre-Hispanic languages, we have reproduced Dr. Van Young's map entitled, "Native Languages of Center-West Mexico in 1519."[4]

But, according to Dr. Van Young, "the extensive and deep-running mestizaje of the area has meant that at any time much beyond the close of the colonial period the history of the native peoples has been progressively interwoven with (or submerged in) that of non-native groups."[5]

---

[4] *Ibid.*, p. 144.

[5] *Ibid.*, p. 138.

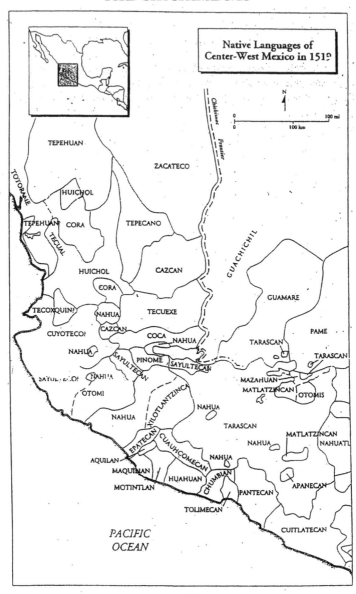

Native Languages of Center-West Mexico in 1519

THE CHICHIMECAS

Unfortunately, our image of pre-Hispanic Jalisco is obscured by the cultural shock, the devastation, and widespread displacement that was inflicted upon the indigenous peoples of western Mexico during the Sixteenth Century. Four primary factors influenced the post-contact indigenous distribution of Jalisco as it evolved into a Spanish colony. These factors are presented below in chronological order:

A. The occupation and conquest of Nuño de Guzmán (1529-1536).

B. The influence of epidemics in reducing the indigenous population.

C. The Mixtón Rebellion (1540-1541).

D. The Chichimeca War (1550-1590)

The Chichimeca Indians

In 1522, shortly after the fall of Tenochtitlán (Mexico City), Hernán Cortés commissioned Cristóbal de Olid to journey into the area now known as Jalisco. In these early days, the Spaniards found it necessary to utilize the services of their new allies, the Christianized sedentary Indians from the south.

THE CHICHIMECAS

These indigenous auxiliaries – serving as scouts and soldiers – were usually Mexica (from Tenochtitlán), Tarascans (from Michoacán), Otomí Indians (from Querétaro and Puebla), Cholulans, or Tlaxcalans. Unlike other Indians, they were permitted to ride horses and to carry side arms as soldiers in the service of Spain.

As the Spaniards and their Amerindian allies from the south made their way north into present-day Jalisco, Guanajuato and Zacatecas, they started to encounter large numbers of nomadic Chichimeca Indians. Philip Wayne Powell – whose *Soldiers, Indians, and Silver: North America's First Frontier War* is the definitive source of information relating to the Chichimeca Indians – referred to Chichimeca as "an all-inclusive epithet" that had "a spiteful connotation."[6]

Utilizing the Náhuatl terms for *dog (chichi)* and *rope (mecatl)*, the Mexica had referred to the Chichimecas literally as "of dog lineage." But some historians have

---

[6] Philip Wayne Powell, *op. cit.*, p. 33.

THE CHICHIMECAS

explained that the word Chichimeca has been subject to various interpretations over the years, including "perros altaneros" (arrogant dogs) and "chupadores de sangre" (blood-suckers). The Spaniards borrowed this designation from their Mexica allies and started to refer to the large stretch Chichimeca territory as *La Gran Chichimeca (the Great Chichimeca)*.

Although Chichimeca was used as an umbrella term for all of the nomadic hunters and gatherers inhabiting this part of Mexico, these indigenous peoples were actually divided into several distinct cultures. On the following page, we have reproduced a map from J. Lloyd Mecham's *Francisco de Ibarra and Nueva Vizcaya*, illustrating the approximate boundaries of the Chichimeca Indian nations of Sixteenth Century.[7]

---

[7] J. Lloyd Mecham, *Francisco de Ibarra and Nueva Vizcaya* (Durham, North Carolina: Duke University Press, 1927).

THE CHICHIMECAS

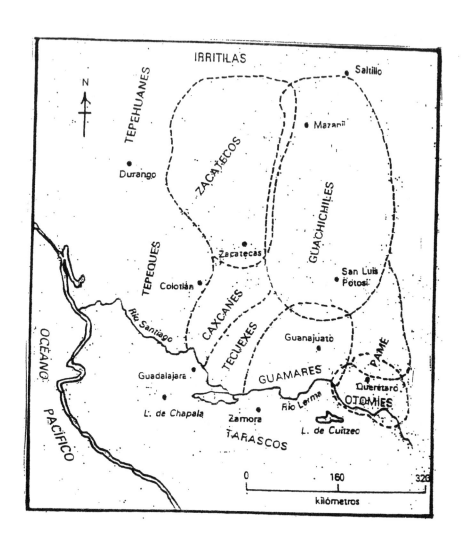

The Chichimeca Nations

THE CHICHIMECAS

Because most of the Chichimeca Indians were rapidly assimilated into the Hispanic culture of Seventeenth Century Mexico, there have been very few historical investigations into their now extinct cultures and languages. Ironically, these indigenous peoples are – in large part – the genetic ancestors of the present-day inhabitants of Guanajuato, Jalisco, Zacatecas, and Aguascalientes. And, as a result, they are thus the ancestors of many Mexican Americans.

The historian Paul Kirchhoff, in his work "The Hunting-Gathering People of North Mexico,"[8] has provided us with the best description of the Chichimeca Indian groups. Most of the Chichimeca Indians shared a primitive hunting-collecting culture, based on the gathering of mesquite, agave, and tunas (the fruit of the nopal). However, many of them also lived off of acorns, roots and seeds.

---

[8] Paul Kirchhoff, "The Hunting-Gathering People of North Mexico," in Basil C. Hedrick et al. (ed.), *The North Mexican Frontier: Readings in Archaeology, Ethnohistory, and Ethnography* (Carbondale, Illinois: Southern Illinois University Press, 1971), pp. 200-209

In some areas, the Chichimecas even cultivated maize and some calabashes. From the mesquite they made white bread and wine. Many Chichimec tribes utilized the juice of the agave as a substitute for water when the latter was in short supply.

The Zacatecos Indians

The Zacatecos Indians, occupying 60,000 square kilometers in the present-day states of Zacatecas, eastern Durango, and Aguascalientes, may have received their name from the Mexica word *zacate* (grass). But some contemporary sources have said that the name was actually taken from the Zacatecos language and that it meant *cabeza negra* ("black head").[9] This would be a reference to the Chichimeca's penchant for painting their bodies and faces with various pigments (in this case, black pigment).

The Zacatecos Indians lived closest to the silver mines that the Spaniards would discover in 1546. The Zacatecos Indians inhabited large portions of northwest and southwest

---

[9] Philip Wayne Powell, *op. cit.*, p. 237.

THE CHICHIMECAS

Zacatecas. Their lands bordered with those of the Tepehuanes on the west and the Guachichiles on the east. They roamed as far north as Parras, where they came into contact with the Irritilas of Coahuila.

The Zacatecos Indians belonged to the Aztecoidan Language Family and were thus of Uto-Aztecan stock. It was believed that the Zacatecos were closely related to the Caxcanes Indians of northern Jalisco and southern Zacatecas.[10]

The Zacatecos were "a tall, well-proportioned, muscular people, their strength being evidenced by the great burdens they carried for the Spaniards." They had oval faces with "long black eyes wide apart, large mouth, thick lips and small flat noses." The men wore breechcloth, while the women wore short petticoats of skins or woven maguey. Both sexes wore their hair long, usually to the waist.[11]

---

[10] John R. Swanton, *The Indian Tribes of North America*, Smthosonian Institution Bureau of American Ethnology Bulletin 145 (Washington, D.C.: Smithsonian Institution Press, 1952), p. 642.

[11] Peter Masten Dunne, *Pioneer Jesuits in Northern Mexico* (Berkeley: University of California Press, 1944), p. 21; J. Lloyd Mecham, *op. cit.*, pp. 62-63.

THE CHICHIMECAS

The Zacatecos Indians married young, with most girls being married by the age of fifteen. Monogamy was their general practice. The Indians smeared their bodies with clay of various colors and painted them with the forms of reptiles. This paint helped shield them from the sun's rays but also kept vermin off their skin.[12]

Some Zacatecos Indians grew roots, herbs, maize, beans, and some wild fruits. Most of them hunted rabbits, deer, birds, frogs, snakes, worms, moles, rats, and reptiles. Eventually, the Zacatecos and some of the other Chichimecas would develop a fondness for the meat of the larger animals brought in by the Spaniards. During their raids on Spanish settlements, they frequently stole mules, horses, cattle, and other livestock, all of which became a part of their diet.

Although most of the Chichimeca Indians were nomadic, some of the Zacatecos Indians had dwellings of a more permanent character, inhabiting areas near the wooded

---

[12] *Ibid.;* Peter Masten Dunne, *op. cit.*, p. 21.

sierras. They inhabited homes constructed of adobe or sun-dried bricks and stones. They slept on the floors of their one-room homes and a fireplace in the middle of the floor, surrounded by rocks, was used for cooking food.[13]

Dr. Powell writes that the Zacatecos were "brave and bellicose warriors and excellent marksmen." They were greatly feared by the neighboring tribes, in particular the Caxcanes, whom they attacked in later years after they began cooperating with the Spaniards.[14]

The Guachichiles

The Guachichile Indians were the most populous Chichimeca nation, occupying perhaps 100,000 square kilometers, from Lake Chapala in Jalisco to modern Saltillo in Coahuila. The Guachichiles inhabited all of eastern Zacatecas and some parts of western San Luis Potosí.

---

[13] *Ibid.*, p. 63.

[14] Philip Wayne Powell, *op. cit.*, p. 39.

THE CHICHIMECAS

The Guachichile Indians were classified with the Aztecoidan division of the Uto-Aztecan linguistic family. It was believed that they were closely related to the Huichol Indians, who continue to live in Nayarit and the western fringes of Zacatecas in the present day era.[15]

The name "Guachichil" was given to them by the Mexica, and meant "head colored red." They had been given this label because "they were distinguished by red feather headdresses, by painting themselves red (especially the hair), or by wearing head coverings (bonetillas) made of hides and painted red."[16]

The archaeologist Paul Kirchhoff wrote that the following traits characterized the Guachichile Indians: "painting of the body; coloration of the hair; head gear; matrilocal residence; freedom of the married woman; special forms of cruelty to enemies."[17]

---

[15] John R. Swanton, *op. cit.*, p. 621.

[16] Philip Wayne Powell, *op. cit.* p. 35; Paul Kirchhoff, *op. cit.*, p. 204.

[17] *Ibid.*, p. 207.

THE CHICHIMECAS

In the development of tribal alliances, the Guachichiles were considered the most advanced of the Chichimec tribes. They were a major catalyst in provoking the other tribes to resist the Spanish settlement and exploitation of Indian lands. "Their strategic position in relation to Spanish mines and highways," wrote Mr. Powell, "made them especially effective in raiding and in escape from Spanish reprisal."[18]

The Spanish frontiersmen and contemporary writers referred to the Guachichiles "as being the most ferocious, the most valiant, and the most elusive" of all their indigenous adversaries. In addition, the Christian missionaries found their language difficult to learn because of its "many sharply variant dialects." As a result, the conversion of these natives to Christianity did not come easy.[19]

---

[18] Philip Wayne Powell, *op. cit.* pp. 35-36.

[19] *Ibid.*

In the development of tribal alliances, the Guachichiles were considered the most advanced of the Chichimec tribes. They were a major catalyst in provoking the other tribes to resist the Spanish settlement and exploitation of Indian lands. "Their strategic position in relation to Spanish mines and highways," wrote Mr. Powell, "made them especially effective in raiding and in escape from Spanish reprisal."[20]

The Guamares

The nation of the Guamares, located in the Guanajuato Sierras, was centered around Pénjamo and San Miguel. They extended as far north as San Felipe, and almost to Querétaro in the east. They also extended as far west as Aguascalientes and Lagos de Moreno. Because many of my Indian ancestors came from Lagos de Moreno, it is highly likely that the Guamare Indians are among my ancestors.[21]

---

[20] *Ibid.*, p. 35.

[21] *Ibid.*, pp. 37-38.

THE CHICHIMECAS

The author, Gonzalo de las Casas, called the Guamares "the bravest, most warlike, treacherous, and destructive of all the Chichimecas, and the most astute (*dispuesta*)." One Guamar group called the "Chichimecas Blancos" lived in the region between Jalostotitlán and Aguascalientes. This branch of the Guamares painted their heads white. However, much like the Guachichiles, many of the Guamares colored their long hair red and painted the body with various colors (in particular red).[22]

The Caxcanes

The Caxcanes Indians were a tribe of the Nahuatlan (Aztecoidan) division of the Uto-Aztecan linguistic stock.[23] Caxcanes Indians occupied portions of present day Aguascalientes, southern Zacatecas and northern Jalisco. Their range – at certain times – extended south toward Lake Chapala and beyond the Río Grande de Santiago.

---

[22] Paul Kirchhoff, *op. cit.*, p. 204; John Wayne Powell, *op. cit.*, pp. 37-38.

[23] John R. Swanton, *op. cit.*, p. 616.

THE CHICHIMECAS

Dr. Phil C. Weigand of the Departmento de Antropología of the Colegio de Michoacán in Mexico has theorized that the Caxcanes Indians probably originated in the Chalchihuites area of northwestern Zacatecas. After the collapse of the Chalchihuites culture around 900 to 1000 A.D., Dr. Weigand believes that "the Caxcanes began a prolonged period of southern expansion" into parts of Jalisco.[24]

Dr. Weigand has further noted that – at the time of the Spanish contact – the Caxcanes "were probably organized into small conquest states" and that the "overriding theme of their history seems to have been a steady expansion carried by warfare, to the south."[25]

Dr. Weigand also observed that the Caxcanes "appear to have been organized into highly competitive, expansion states. These states possessed well-developed social hierarchies, monumental architecture, and military

---

[24] Phil C. Weigand, *op. cit.,* p. 169.

[25] *Ibid.*

brotherhoods." The Caxcanes are believed to have built their primary peñoles (fortifications) and religious centers at Juchípila, Teúl, Teocaltiche, Tlatenango, Nochistlán, Jalpa and El Chique.[26]

The Caxcanes played a major role in both the Mixton Rebellion (1540-41) and the Chichimeca War (1550-1590), first as the adversaries of the Spaniards and later as their allies against the Zacatecos and Guachichiles. The *cocolistle* epidemic of 1584 greatly reduced the number of Caxcanes. In the decades to follow, the surviving Caxcanes assimilated into the more dominant cultures that had settled in their territory. Today, Dr. Weigand writes, "the Caxcanes no longer exist as an ethnic group" and that "their last survivors" were noted in the late 1890s.[27]

Nuño de Guzmán

In December 1529, Nuño de Guzman, left Mexico City at the head of a force of five hundred Spaniards and 10,000

---

[26] *Ibid.*, pp. 170-171

[27] *Ibid.*, pp. 175.

Indian allies. According to J. Lloyd Mecham, the author of *Francisco de Ibarra and Nueva Vizcaya,*[28] "Guzmán was an able and even brilliant lawyer, a man of great energy and firmness, but insatiably ambitious, aggressive, wily, and cruel." As the Governor of the First Audencia of Mexico, his ruthless and cruel practices would antagonize both the indigenous populations and his fellow Spaniards. His cruelty towards the Amerindians would have important repercussions and lead directly to the Mixtón Rebellion of 1540.

In a rapid and brutal campaign lasting from February to June, 1520, Guzmán traveled through Michoacán, Jalisco, and southern Zacatecas. Although other Spanish explorers had already discovered these areas, Guzmán ignored prior rights of discovery by provoking the natives to revolt so that he might subdue them. The historian Peter Gerhard writes that "Guzmán's strategy throughout was to terrorize the natives with often unprovoked killing, torture, and enslavement – there was remarkably little resistance. The

---

[28] J. Lloyd Mecham, *op. cit.*, p. 22.

army left a path of corpses and destroyed houses and crops, impressing surviving males into service and leaving women and children to starve."[29]

Taking formal possession of the conquered areas, Guzmán named this region "Greater Spain." However, twelve years later, a Spanish court ordered that the land should be renamed Nueva Galicia (New Galicia). This new territory took in parts of the present-day states of Zacatecas, Jalisco, Aguascalientes, and San Luis Potosí.

Guzmán's treatment of the Indians earned him the nickname of "Bloody Guzmán." The actions of this man would stir up hatred and resentment that would haunt the Spaniards for decades to come. In January, 1532, Guzmán founded Guadalajara, naming the city after his place of birth in Spain. However, the small settlement came under Indian attack almost immediately and had to be abandoned in August 1533. The city would be founded at a new

---

[29] *Ibid.*, p. 23; Peter Gerhard, *The North Frontier of New Spain* (Princeton: Princeton University Press, 1982), pp. 42-43.

location a few years later. In the meantime, reports of Guzmán's brutal treatment of the indigenous people got the attention of the authorities in Mexico City. In 1536, Guzmán was arrested and impiisoned. In 1538, his trial was removed to Spain, where he would die in poverty and disgrace six years later.

The Mixtón Rebellion

The historian Philip Wayne Powell writes that "the dream of great wealth to be found somewhere in interior Mexico tantalized explorers and conquerors."[30] The most intriguing legend of all was the myth surrounding the Seven Cities of Cibola. In February 1540, Francisco Vásquez de Coronado set out from Compostela with an exploratory force of 336 well-armed Spanish soldiers, a thousand horses and swine, and hundreds of Indian allies in search of the fabled cities of gold.

After Coronado's army departed for the north, the small Spanish settlements that existed in Jalisco and Zacatecas

---

[30] Philip Wayne Powell, *op. cit.*, p. 3.

became restless. Coronado's expedition had left the frontier area of Nueva Galicia sparsely populated. With the Spanish garrisons seriously undermanned, the settlers feared a general insurrection of the native peoples. Their fears were not unfounded. The natives, still reeling from Guzmán's genocidal bloodbath of a decade earlier, harbored great resentment towards the European invaders and waited for the opportunity to take on the Spanish intruders and their Indian allies. Their goal: the complete expulsion of all the strangers from their territory.

The first hostilities began in the spring of 1540, with the murder of Juan de Arce by the Guaynamota Indians of his encomienda. Soon after, other uprisings took place in the hills near Teul and Nochistlán and along the coastal region. Everywhere, friars and encomenderos were attacked by their charges. By April of 1541, the Caxcanes of southern Zacatecas and northern Jalisco were waging a full-scale revolt against all symbols of Spanish rule.

Hearing news of this dangerous rebellion, Pedro de Alvarado, the friend of Cortés and conqueror of Guatemala, hastened to Guadalajara in June 1541 with a force of 400 men. Refusing to await reinforcements, Alvarado led a direct attack against the Juchipila Indians near Nochistlán. On June 24, several thousand Indians attacked the Spaniards with such ferocity that they were forced to retreat with heavy losses. In this retreat, Alvarado was crushed when he fell under his horse. He died in Guadalajara from his injuries on July 4, 1541.

It took almost two years to contain the Mixtón Rebellion. Antonio de Mendoza, who had become the first Viceroy of Nueva España in 1535, quickly assembled a force of 450 Spaniards and some 30,000 Aztec and Tlaxcalan auxiliaries. In a series of short sieges and assaults, Mendoza captured the native fortresses one by one. By December 1541, the native resistance had been completely crushed. A few months later, the Coronado Expedition returned to Mexico City empty-handed, having failed to locate the Seven Cities of Cibola.

Although the Spaniards had won the war, the Mixtón Rebellion had a profound effect upon the Spanish expansion in central and northern Mexico. The historian J. Lloyd Mecham observed that "the uprising in Nueva Galicia not only checked advance in that direction, but even caused a temporary contraction of the frontiers."[31]

However, as serious as this insurrection was, it was merely a prelude to a more fierce and protracted struggle. The Chichimeca Indians – considered so inferior to Spanish and Mexica culture – would defend their homeland with a ferocity that few could imitate.

---

[31] *Ibid.*, p.34

A FRONTIER UNDER SIEGE

The Zacatecas mines became the focal point for the realization of the great dream of quick wealth... Zacatecas was the center of the boom, the symbol and the goal of the northward sweep. Unfortunately... one serious problem became quickly apparent. The rush to Zacatecas left in its wake a long stretch of unsettled and unexplored territory...[1]

As their territory began to be occupied by Spanish settlers and stock raisers, they [the Chichimeca Indians] resisted the intrusion in the most obvious way open to them – assault on travelers and merchants using the roads. So began the 'Guerra de los Chichimecas,' the longest and most expensive conflict between Spaniards and the indigenous peoples of New Spain in the history of the colony.[2]

An Elusive Enemy

For at least three centuries, my ancestors in northern Jalisco lived, worked, and served under the flags of Spain and Mexico. As Christians, they baptized their children and took their marriage vows in the Catholic churches that the Spaniards had built on their ancestral lands. And, today, this region is a land of peace and moderate prosperity.

---

[1] Philip Wayne Powell, *op. cit.*, p. 14.

[2] P.J. Bakewell, *Silver Mining and Society in Colonial Mexico: Zacatecas, 1546-1700.* (Cambridge: Cambridge University Press, 1971), p. 22.

However, in the Sixteenth Century, as the Spaniards started to infiltrate their native lands, my indigenous ancestors resisted with a ferocity that became legendary. For half a century, the Spanish military waged a frustrating war against an elusive enemy. The story of this resistance is a story that has not been told in very many American books. But I shall tell the story here.

The aftermath of the Mixtón Rebellion led to great suffering for the Caxcanes and other Indians in the highlands north of Guadalajara. Viceroy Mendoza's response to the rebellion was brutal. Peter Gerhard writes that "thousands were killed, thousands starved to death, thousands were driven off in chains to the mines, and many of the survivors (mostly women and children) were transported from their homelands to work on Spanish farms and haciendas." A plague, lasting from 1545 to 1548, killed off half of the surviving Indians.[3]

---

[3] Peter Gerhard, *op. cit.*, p. 49.

A FRONTIER UNDER SIEGE

The Discovery of Silver in Zacatecas

On September 8, 1546, Juan de Tolosa, a Basque of noble heritage, led a small force of Spaniards and Indian auxiliaries into the vicinity of the present-day city of Zacatecas. Accompanied by four Franciscan friars, Tolosa made friendly approaches to the local natives, who handed the Spaniards stones, which were later determined to be silver.

Subsequently, the Indians took Tolosa to the location of the ore deposits. This encounter led to the founding of the city of Zacatecas deep within the territory of the Chichimeca Indians, some 618 kilometers (384 miles) northwest of Mexico City and 315 kilometers (196 miles) northeast of Guadalajara. In the next few years, Spanish entrepreneurs would make their way to Zacatecas to locate and exploit rich mineral deposits that seemed to dot the landscape of this semi-arid region.

The discovery of rich mineral-bearing deposits in this area put the spotlight on Zacatecas. The spotlight grew wider as other deposits were discovered farther north: San Martín (1556), Chalchihuites (1556), Avino (1558), Sombrerete (1558), Fresnillo (1566), Mazapil (1568), and Nieves (1574). "The growth of Zacatecas was phenomenal," writes J. Lloyd Mecham, "The news of the rich discoveries spread rapidly, and soon the region was crowded with treasure seekers..."[4]

Although the Spaniards were the primary beneficiaries of the silver strike, most of the mineworkers were not Spanish. Indian labor and African slaves would provide the muscle needed to extract the silver ore from the mines. The Spaniards had brought with them their Indian allies – the Tarascans, Aztecs, Tlaxcalans, and Otomíes – all of whom would supply labor for the mines. Many Caxcanes who had been enslaved after the Mixtón War were also forced to work in the mines.

Viceroy Mendoza's use of Indian auxiliaries to put down the insurrection also brought many Indian laborers into the

---

[4] J. Lloyd Mecham, *op. cit.*, p.46.

area of the silver strikes. Some of the earliest remnants of
Mendoza's forces from the Mixtón Rebellion went to work
as laborers in the Zacatecas mines.

The Chichimeca War

Philip Wayne Powell has observed that "the rush to
Zacatecas left in its wake a long stretch of unsettled and
unexplored territory." The small mining camps adjacent to
the silver mines represented "an isolated nucleus of
Spanish settlement in a surrounding vastness of unknown
lands and peoples."[5]

The strategic location of the Zacatecas mines made
confrontation with the Chichimec Indians inevitable. "The
rush of treasure-seekers and the opening of cart-roads from
central Mexico to these mines," explains Mr. Gerhard, led
to a "displacement of desert tribes" that brought on "a
fierce struggle (the Chichimec war) that kept the northern

---

[5] Philip Wayne Powell, *op. cit.*, pp. 14-16.

frontier aflame from sea to sea for four decades (1550-1590)."[6]

As the settlements and the mineral output of the mines grew in numbers, "the needs of transport to and from" the mining area became "a vital concern of miners, merchants, and government." To function properly, the Zacatecas silver mines "required well-defined and easily traveled routes." These routes brought in badly needed supplies and equipment from distant towns and also delivered the silver to smelters and royal counting houses in the south.[7]

Mr. Powell wrote that "the highways... became the tangible, most frequently visible evidence of the white man's permanent intrusion in the land of the Chichimecas." This increasingly heavy traffic on the highways attracted the attention of the Chichimecs. As the settlements expanded and new roads were paved, the traffic on these highways came into the view of more tribes. As the natives

---

[6] Peter Gerhard, *op. cit.*, p. 6.

[7] Philip Wayne Powell, *op.cit.*, p. 16.

learned about the usefulness of the goods being transported (silver, food, and clothing), "they quickly appreciated the vulnerability of this highway movement to any attack they might launch."[8]

Thus, the stage was set for the Chichimec War. In 1550, the first strikes were made by Zacatecos Indians who attacked caravans south of the town of Zacatecas. But, soon after, the Guachichiles farther south made even more destructive attacks on the new roads through the Guanajuato Sierras. It is believed that about 120 people were killed in the first months of the war.

In the years to follow, the majority of the attacks were aimed primarily at highway traffic to and from the new silver mines and at *estancias* (small cattle ranches) in or near the edge of the *tierra de guerra* (Land of War). In most cases, the Indians prepared their attack in a narrow pass or in rocky and broken terrain, at the mouth of a ravine, or in a place with sufficient forestation to conceal their approach. They usually ambushed their victims at

---

[8] *Ibid.*, pp. 16-17.

dawn or dusk and struck with great speed. Mr. Powell wrote that "surprise, nudity, body paint, shouting, and rapid shooting were all aimed at terrifying the intended victims and their animals. There is ample evidence that they usually succeeded in this."[9]

In writing about the Chichimec way of life, Mr. Powell refers to these Indians as "an elusive enemy, highly dangerous in expert use of bow and arrow and in knowledge of the land on which he fought." Spaniards and Indians alike dreaded close combat with the Chichimeca warrior. "In hand-to-hand combat," explains Mr. Powell, "the Chichimeca warrior gained, among other Indians and Spaniards, a reputation for courage and ferocity."[10]

Mr. Powell also writes that even when the Chichimeca warrior was cornered he remained a dangerous foe:[11]

---

[9] *Ibid.*, pp. 45-46.

[10] *Ibid.*, pp. 44-46.

[11] *Ibid.*, p. 46.

> When the Chichimeca was attacked in his
> mountainous or other naturally protected
> stronghold or hideout, he usually put up vigorous
> resistance, especially if unable to escape the
> onslaught. In such cases, he fought – with
> arrows, clubs, or even rocks – behind natural
> barriers (or in caves) that had sometimes been
> made stronger by his own hands and ingenuity.
> Even the women might take up the fight, using
> the weapons of fallen braves. The warriors did
> not readily surrender and were known to fight on
> with great strength even after receiving mortal
> wounds.

The encampments of the Chichimecas were "difficult to access, often hidden in caves, ravines, and small valleys with mountain, forest, or rocky terrain as protective features." And eventually, the Chichimecas learned how to utilize the horse in warfare. "Once on horseback," Mr. Powell explains, "he [the Chichimeca warrior] was exceedingly dangerous."[12]

In addition to using a horse to mount his attacks, the Chichimeca warrior's primary weapon was the bow and

---

[12] *Ibid.*, pp. 46, 50.

arrow, and, as Mr. Powell wrote, "his skillful use of it was a cause of wonderment and fear among his Spanish and Indian adversaries. The warrior could release arrows with rapidity greater than Spanish manipulation of harquebus or crossbow."[13]

The intensity of the attacks increased with each year. According to Mr. Powell, in one five year period (1552-1556), Chichimeca attacks in the Jilotepec province killed more than three hundred peaceful natives in the pueblo and vicinity of Jalpa alone.[14] But the worst disaster of all occurred in 1554 when a train of sixty wagons with an armed escort was attacked by the Chichimecas in the Ojuelos Pass. In addition to inflicting great loss of life, the Chichimecas carried off more than 30,000 pesos worth of clothing, silver, and other valuables.[15]

---

[13] *Ibid.*, p. 47.

[14] *Ibid.*, p. 60.

[15] *Ibid.*, p. 61.

A FRONTIER UNDER SIEGE

By the end of 1561, an estimated 200 Spaniards and more than 2,000 Indian allies and traders had been killed on the roads between Guadalajara, Michoacan, Mexico, and the northern mines. Property damage was estimated at more than one million gold pesos, while the loss in royal wagons and treasure was estimated at 400,000 gold pesos.[16]

Knowledge of their fate at the hands of the Chichimeca had a profound psychological effect upon settlers, travelers, merchants, and missionaries. Many decided to abandon the frontier life altogether. The result was depopulation of the mining camps and estancias. In addition, the Spanish administrators had great difficulty in recruiting soldiers who were willing to go after the Chichimecas in reprisal unless the captured enemy could be subjected to slavery.

Although slavery of captured Indians was officially outlawed, enforcement of such laws became lax. Spanish military authorities came to realize that they would never be able to carry on an effective war against the Chichimecs

---

[16] *Ibid.*

unless the Spanish soldiers were able to procure Indian labor as a reward for military services. In 1560, the official policy changed, providing that Indian captives should be deposited (with those making the capture) for a period of six years "more or less."

As the Chichimec War continued, the Spanish authorities reported that many ranchos and mining centers were being abandoned. The population of the small settlement of Aguascalientes, founded on October 22, 1575, dwindled to one captain, 16 soldiers, and two civilian residents during the 1582-85 period. By 1585, official reports were stating that highway travel beyond the city of Zacatecas to the more northern mines was all but nonexistent.

Pacification and Peace

If there was any single date that represented a turning of the tide in the Chichimec War, it would be October 18, 1885. On this day, Alonso Manrique de Zuñiga, the Marqués de Villamanrique, became the seventh viceroy of Mexico. Mr. Powell writes that "to this great viceroy must go the major share of credit for planning and largely effecting the end" of the war and "the development of basic policies to guarantee a sound pacification of the northern frontier." He evaluated the deteriorating situation, consulted expert advice, and reversed the practices of the past.[17]

The Viceroy learned that many Spanish soldiers had begun raiding peaceful Indians for the purpose of enslavement. Infuriated by this practice, the Marqués prohibited further enslavement of all captured Indians and freed or placed under religious care those who had already been captured.[18]

The Viceroy also appointed Don Antonio de Monroy to conduct investigations into this conduct and punish the Spaniards involved in the slave trade. Through his inquiries, Marqués de Villamanrique found that the bulk of the Spanish military expenditures had been badly mismanaged and had failed to eliminate the Indian threat. He eliminated unauthorized military expeditions into the

---

[17] *Ibid.*, pp. 183-184.

[18] *Ibid.*, pp. 184-185.

Gran Chichimeca and reduced the number of garrisons and troops serving in the war zone.[19]

Villamanrique also launched a full-scale peace offensive. He opened negotiations with the principal Chichimeca leaders, and, according to Mr. Powell, made to them "promises of food, clothing, lands, religious administration, and agricultural implements to attract them to peaceful settlement." As it turns out, the olive branch proved to be more persuasive than the sword, and on November 25, 1589, the Viceroy was able to report to the King that the state of war had ended. [20]

The policy of peace by persuasion was continued under the next Viceroy, Luis de Velasco. He sent Franciscan and Jesuit missionaries into the former war zone and spent more money on food and agricultural tools for the Chichimecas. He also recruited some 400 families of

---

[19] *Ibid.*, pp. 185-186.

[20] *Ibid.*, pp. 185-190.

Tlaxcalans from the south and settled them in eight towns of the war zone.

Velasco's successor, the Conde de Monterrey, completed Velasco's work by establishing a language school at Zacatecas to teach missionaries the various Chichimeca dialects. Through this effort, the conversion of the Chichimeca Indians to Christianity would be streamlined. Having learned how to communicate with the Chichimecs, many missionaries became important diplomats of peace during this period.

The most important component of the "peace by purchase" policy involved the shipment and distribution of food, clothing, and agricultural implements to four strategically located depots (*almacenes*). The clothing shipped, according to Mr. Powell, included coarse woolen cloth (*sayal*), coarse blankets in mixed colors, Castilian blankets, woven petticoats, shirts, hats and capes. The agricultural implements included plows, hoes, axes, hatchets, leather saddles, and slaughtering knives.[21]

After the turn of the century, the continuing purchase of peace by food and clothing tied the now-sedentary Indians to the Spanish system. It is also important to remember that most of these Amerindians had been granted exemption from forced service and tribute and had thus retained their independence of action.[22]

Who Are My Ancestors?

The lands of Zacatecas and Jalisco gave birth to my family. All of my ancestors come from this part of Mexico. My maternal ancestors, the Dominguez family, came from the municipio of Sain Alto in northwestern Zacatecas. This would give me a high proportion of Zacatecos Indians, who dominated that region.

---

[21] *Ibid.*, pp. 218-219.

[22] *Ibid.*, p. 219.

A FRONTIER UNDER SIEGE

My paternal ancestors, the Morales and Luevano families, are of mixed stock. Several of my father's maternal ancestors came from Spain to Aguascalientes, while others are believed to have been descended from African slaves who married into Spanish and Indian families.

As the large numbers of indigenous peoples throughout Mexico started to die from European diseases or mistreatment, African slaves were brought in to assume a significant share of the labor. For example, in 1576-1577, some 2,500 Indians in the City of Zacatecas perished during the devastating *matlazahuatl* epidemic (probably typhus). Having lost a significant proportion of the mining labor force, the Spanish authorities found it necessary to bring in an increasing number of African slaves from central Mexico to alleviate the labor shortage.

My father's direct Morales line and its collateral extensions, which are predominantly Indian, came almost entirely from Lagos de Moreno in northeastern corner of the present-day state of Jalisco. In Indian times, Lagos de Moreno was called Pechichitán and later Chichimequillas.

It is believed that the lands of the Caxcanes, Tecuexes, Guachichiles and Guamares all intersected near Lagos. For this reason, it may be assumed that the blood of all four tribes runs through my veins. All four indigenous groups, like the Zacatecos Indians, were members of the Uto-Aztecoidan linguistic family.

Exploring the names of the Indian tribes who lived in the vicinity of my ancestral lands helps us answer part of the question, "Who are my ancestors?" But the population of Nueva España and Nueva Galicia, during the first two hundred years (1521-1721) was in a constant state of flux. The primary instigator of the enormous and wide-ranging migration and resettlement patterns in Mexico was Spain's frequent use of Indians as soldiers, slaves, or settlers (*pobladores*).

In describing this phenomenon, Mr. Powell noted that "Indians formed the bulk of the fighting forces against the

Chichimeca warriors." Continuing with this reflection, Mr. Powell writes:[23]

> *As fighters, as burden bearers, as interpreters, as scouts, as emissaries, the pacified natives of New Spain played significant and often indispensable roles in subjugating and civilizing the Chichimeca country. Occasionally armies composed exclusively of these native warriors (particularly the Otomies) roamed the tierra de guerra to seek out, defeat, and help Christianize the hostile nomad of the north. On some parts of the frontier defense against Chichimeca attacks was at times exclusively in the hands of the native population... Spanish authority and personnel were in most cases supervising agents for manpower supplied by Indian allies. The white men were the organizers of the effort; native allies did much of the hard work and often bore the brunt of the fighting. In the early years of the war the Spaniards placed heavy reliance upon those natives who had been wholly or partly subdued by the Cortesian conquest – Mexicans, Tarascans, Otomies, among others.*
>
> *This use of native allies... led eventually to a virtual disappearance of the nomadic tribes as*

---

[23] Philip Wayne Powell, *op. cit.,* pp. 158-159.

they were absorbed into the northward-moving Tarascans, Aztecs, Cholultecans, Otomíes, Tlaxcalans, Cazcanes, and others... within a few decades of the general pacification at the end of the century the Guachichiles, Zacatecos, Guamares, and other tribes or nations were disappearing as distinguishable entities in the Gran Chichimeca.

And thus, Mr. Powell concludes, "the sixteenth-century land of war thus became fully Mexican in its mixture." Many of these Aztecs, Tlaxcalans, Cholulans, Otomíes, and Tarascans came to the Zacatecas mining camps and "hired themselves out to Spanish employers, mainly to dig and carry ore."[24]

War, settlements, agriculture, the mining industry, encomiendas, and slavery have all contributed to major population movements that transformed, displaced and integrated the pre-Hispanic Indian population of Mexico. As a result, many areas of Mexico lost their homogeneous character. This appears to be the case for the lands from which my ancestors came. Therefore, the answer to my

---

[24] P. J. Bakewell, in *Provinces of Early Mexico*, p. 215.

question (Who are my ancestors?) is, "All the Indians of Mexico are my ancestors."

LAGOS DE MORENO

For the Spanish it was of utmost importance to vanquish the Chichimec people, who posed a military threat because they inhabited thousands of villages in the territories bordering the Valley of Mexico... it was also necessary to conquer the Chichimec villages because they obstructed the Spaniards' northward movement.[1]

As... enticement to side with Spain, Indians were given tools, cooking utensils, and clothing. Through this divide and conquer process the Spanish gradually gained support from some Indian groups and began to move further north, each village becoming a stepping stone in the northern invasion.[2]

The Surname Morales

The surname Morales is derived from *moral*, the Spanish word for mulberry tree, specifically the Black European Mulberry. The suffix "es" or "ez" in Spanish denotes "son of." So I presume that a person who was called Morales in Medieval Spain may have been a person who dwelt near a mulberry tree. However, in the Spanish language, *moral* also means "moral." Therefore, it is equally possible that

---

[1] Martha Menchaca, *Recovering History, Constructing Race: The Indian, Black, and White Roots of Mexican Americans* (Austin: University of Texas Press, 2001), p. 69.

[2] *Ibid.*

99

Morales may also have designated a person who is right and true. This interpretation has great meaning for me because my father, Daniel Morales, was a very moral and very righteous person.

It has been said that the surname Morales originated in Santander in northwest Spain sometime around the Eleventh Century. For many years, I wondered to myself, "When did my first Morales ancestor come to Mexico from Spain. And from what part of Spain did he come from?" I had thought that it would be very interesting to find out that some distant Morales ancestor had left some part of Spain, perhaps in the hopes of coming to Mexico to make his fortune. Since most of us Mexican Americans carry Spanish surnames that would be a logical presumption.

A Family of Indians

However, family history research has determined that my earliest Morales ancestors on my direct paternal line were Indians from the town of Lagos de Moreno in the northern highlands of Jalisco. My great-great-great-great-great-great-grandparents, Miguel Morales and María de la Cruz, were

LAGOS DE MORENO

Indian peasants who were raising their family during the last two decades of the Seventeenth Century. On the following page is a chart showing the line of descent from Miguel Morales – the indigenous peasant – to the present generation of Morales descendants.

I have been able to trace my father's direct paternal line back to the Seventeenth Century because the Catholic church parish registers (*Registros Parroquiales*) go back to 1634. I was able to access the baptism and marriage records for many of my ancestors because they are available through the Family History Library of Salt Lake City, which permits individuals of any religious persuasion to access their huge collection of parish registers. The Parish registers of Lagos de Moreno range from 1634 to 1957 and can be accessed on 476 rolls of microfilm.[3]

---

[3] The primary rolls of microfilm that contained the baptisms of my ancestors at Lagos de Moreno from 1634 to 1803 were Rolls 221404 through 221423. Most of the marriage records I consulted were found on Rolls 221512 through 221519 (Salt Lake City, Utah: Sociedad Genealógica de Utah, 1958)

LAGOS DE MORENO

1. Miguel Morales
sp: Maria de la Cruz
└ 2. Juan Morales (b.1698-Lagos de Moreno)
  sp: Paula Petrona de la Cruz (b.1705-Lagos de Moreno;m.1722)
  └ 3. Francisco Xavier Morales (b.1725-Lagos de Moreno)
    sp: Lucrecia Rosalia Montelongo (b.1735-Lagos de Moreno;m.1754)
    └ 4. Jose Nosiforo Morales (b.1755-Lagos de Moreno)
      sp: Maria Josefa Delgado (b.1776-Lagos de Moreno;m.1794)
      └ 5. Jose Casimiro Morales (b.1804-Moreno de los Lagos)
        sp: Zeferina Valades (b.1818-Ojuelos,Jalisco;m.1836)
        └ 6. Austacio Morales (b.1845-Aguascalientes)
          sp: Juana Salas (b.1849-Aguascalientes;m.1873)
          └ 7. Olayo Morales (b.1875-Aguascalientes)
            sp: Juana Luevano (b.1885-Villa Hidalgo,Jalisco;m.1903;d.1951)
            └ 8. Daniel Morales (b.1914-Houston,Texas)
              sp: Pabla Bessie Dominguez (b.1915-Canadian,Texas;m.1937)
              └ 9. Donna Morales (b.1947-Kansas City,KS)
                sp: David Stewart
                ├ 10. Randy Stewart (b.1966-Kansas City,KS)
                │   sp: Betsy Gantt
                │ ├ 11. David Stewart (b.1988-Kansas City,KS)
                │ └ 11. Danielle Stewart (b.1989-Kansas City,KS)
                └ 10. Gina Stewart (b.1969-Kansas City,KS)
                  sp: James Herzog
                  ├ 11. Christian Stewart (b.1992-Killeen,Texas)
                  └ 11. Charlie Herzog (b.1995-Killeen,Texas)

Descendancy Chart – Miguel Morales to the Present Day

LAGOS DE MORENO

The Family History Library owns more than 154,000 rolls of microfilm for all of Mexico. On these rolls of microfilm you can access civil registration records, Catholic church records, local census lists, notarial and land records, and military records. Wherever you may be in the United States, it is possible for you to go to any of the 1,400 Family History Centers and use their facilities to do Mexican genealogical research.

A significant number of ancestors on my direct paternal line appear to have originated among the indigenous inhabitants of the present-day municipio of Lagos de Moreno. On the following page is a pedigree chart illustrating five generations of ancestors of José Casimiro Morales, my great-great-grandfather. Nearly all of these people were born or married in Lagos de Moreno. Only one person on this chart – Josefa de la Peña – is believed to have been of pure Spanish descent. The rest were classified as *indios* (Indians), *mestizos*, and *mulatos*. These classifications will be discussed in greater detail in the next chapter.

LAGOS DE MORENO

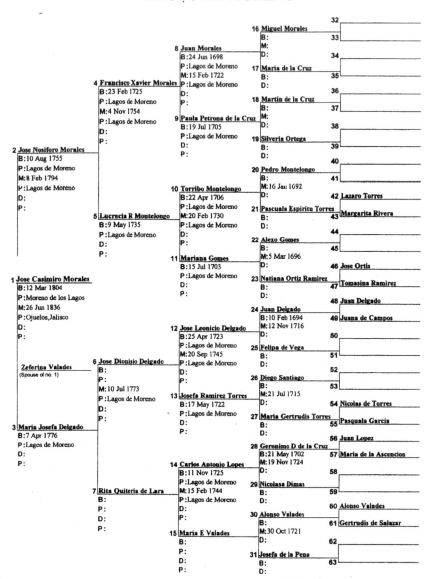

2 Jose Nosiforo Morales
B: 10 Aug 1755
P: Lagos de Moreno
M: 8 Feb 1794
P: Lagos de Moreno
D:
P:

1 Jose Casimiro Morales
B: 12 Mar 1804
P: Moreno de los Lagos
M: 26 Jun 1836
P: Ojuelos, Jalisco
D:
P:

Zeferina Valades
(Spouse of no. 1)

3 Maria Josefa Delgado
B: 7 Apr 1776
P: Lagos de Moreno
D:
P:

4 Francisco Xavier Morales
B: 23 Feb 1725
P: Lagos de Moreno
M: 4 Nov 1754
P: Lagos de Moreno
D:
P:

5 Lucrecia R Montelongo
B: 9 May 1735
P: Lagos de Moreno
D:
P:

6 Jose Dionisio Delgado
B:
P:
M: 10 Jul 1773
P: Lagos de Moreno
D:
P:

7 Rita Quiteria de Lara
B:
P:
D:
P:

8 Juan Morales
B: 24 Jun 1698
P: Lagos de Moreno
M: 15 Feb 1722
P: Lagos de Moreno
D:
P:

9 Paula Petrona de la Cruz
B: 19 Jul 1705
P: Lagos de Moreno
D:
P:

10 Torribo Montelongo
B: 22 Apr 1706
P: Lagos de Moreno
M: 20 Feb 1730
P: Lagos de Moreno
D:
P:

11 Mariana Gomes
B: 15 Jul 1703
P: Lagos de Moreno
D:
P:

12 Jose Leonicio Delgado
B: 25 Apr 1723
P: Lagos de Moreno
M: 20 Sep 1745
P: Lagos de Moreno
D:
P:

13 Josefa Ramirez Torres
B: 17 May 1722
P: Lagos de Moreno
D:
P:

14 Carlos Antonio Lopes
B: 11 Nov 1725
P: Lagos de Moreno
M: 15 Feb 1744
P: Lagos de Moreno
D:
P:

15 Maria E Valades
B:
P:
D:
P:

16 Miguel Morales
B:
M:
D:

17 Maria de la Cruz
B:
D:

18 Martin de la Cruz
B:
M:
D:

19 Silveria Ortega
B:
D:

20 Pedro Montelongo
B:
M: 16 Jan 1692
D:

21 Pascuala Espiritu Torres
B:
D:

22 Alexo Gomes
B:
M: 5 Mar 1696
D:

23 Natiana Ortiz Ramirez
B:
D:

24 Juan Delgado
B: 10 Feb 1694
M: 12 Nov 1716
D:

25 Felipa de Vega
B:
D:

26 Diego Santiago
B:
M: 21 Jul 1715
D:

27 Maria Gertrudis Torres
B:
D:

28 Geronimo D de la Cruz
B: 21 May 1702
M: 19 Nov 1724
D:

29 Nicolasa Dimas
B:
D:

30 Alonso Valades
B:
M: 30 Oct 1721
D:

31 Josefa de la Pena
B:
D:

32

33

34

35

36

37

38

39

40

41

42 Lazaro Torres
43 Margarita Rivera

44

45

46 Jose Ortis
47 Tomasina Ramirez

48 Juan Delgado
49 Juana de Campos

50

51

52

53

54 Nicolas de Torres
55 Pasquala Garcia

56 Juan Lopez
57 Maria de la Ascencion

58

59

60 Alonso Valades
61 Gertrudis de Salazar

62

63

Pedigree Chart of José Casimiro Morales

LAGOS DE MORENO

Today, Lagos de Moreno is located in the northeastern part of the Mexican state of Jalisco. It is bounded on the north and west by the municipio of Ojuelos and the state of Aguascalientes, both of which were also home to many of my ancestors. Lagos de Moreno is also bordered on the east by the state of Guanajuato and on the south and west by the municipios of San Juan de Los Lagos and Encarnación de Díaz.

It is interesting to note that the state of Jalisco received its name from the fusion of two Nahuatl words, *xalli* (sand or gravel) and *ixtli* (meaning face, or by extension, plane). Thus, Jalisco can be translated as meaning "sandy plain."

Lagos de Moreno is located about 200 kilometers (125 miles) northeast of Guadalajara and 445 kilometers (275 miles) from Mexico City and is one of the most populous municipios of Jalisco with a population of at least 100,000.

Indigenous Inhabitants

Where Lagos de Moreno stands today was once an Indian village called *Pechichitlán*. According to some sources, the tribe that inhabited the area when the Spaniards arrived was called the *Ixtachichimeca.* I am both intrigued and fascinated to think that many of my ancestors probably belonged to this population center.

Peter Gerhard writes that "most if not all of the region [around Lagos] was occupied at contact by Chichimec hunter-gatherers, probably Guachichiles, with a sprinkling of Guamares in the east." But numerous studies and accounts also mention the presence of both Caxcanes and Tecuexes in the areas immediately to the west of Lagos.[4] As a matter of fact, several of the major religious centers of the Caxcanes were located immediately to the west of Lagos in such locations as Teocaltiche and Nochistlán.

On the following page, our illustrator, Eddie Martinez, has created a map entitled "Indian Languages of Northern Jalisco." In this illustration, Eddie has outlined the approximate boundaries of the various indigenous groups in this area.

---

[4] Peter Gerhard, *op. cit.*, pp. 104-105.

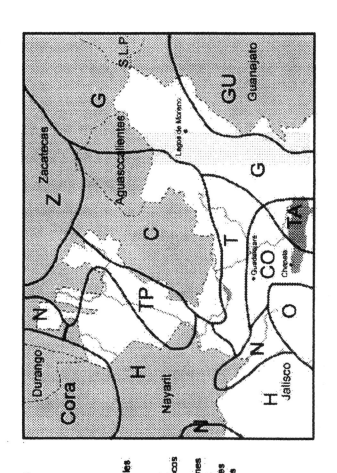

Indian Languages of Northern Jalisco

LAGOS DE MORENO

However, it is important to point out that there is a great deal of contrast between our rigid modern day borders and the Sixteenth Century frontiers among indigenous groups. Today's boundaries are carefully surveyed and mapped. But the boundaries of five centuries ago existed only as fluctuating spheres of influence. As the balance of power shifted from one tribe to another, so too did the territories. And when the Spaniards arrived in this area, they totally altered the delicate balance that had existed between neighboring and rival tribes for centuries.

The delicate balance in the Lagos area was upset in March 1530, when Nuño de Guzmán's lieutenant, Pedro Almíndez Chirinos, with a force of fifty Spaniards and 500 Tarascans and Tlaxcalans, appeared in the area. This army was given a peaceful reception by the Indian inhabitants of the area. Most of Jalisco, however, was ravaged by Guzmán's forces.[5]

During the Mixtón Rebellion of 1540, the Caxcanes Indians living in this region rose in rebellion against the Spanish

---

[5] See pages 69 through 72 in the text of this work.

military authorities. In a desperate attempt to drive the Spaniards from their native lands, the Cazcan Indians burned several churches and killed Christian missionaries. After the Mixtón Rebellion was put down in 1541, cattlemen from Guadalajara started to run their herds through the entire Los Altos region, which had been given the name *Los Lanos* (The Flatlands).

In 1560, the silver mines at Comanja were discovered. Three years later, on January 15, 1563, as the Chichimec War raged throughout the region, the Spanish administration at Guadalajara authorized the founding of Lagos in order to consolidate the position of the Spanish military in this area. A few years earlier, in 1554, the Spanish military had suffered a disastrous defeat in the Ojuelos Pass, north of Lagos.

Charged with the task of establishing the town, Hernando de Martell assembled seventy-three families of settlers. Living south of the newly founded settlement were the Cazcanes, who had aroused such fear during the Mixtón Rebellion of 1541.[6]

Because of the many lakes in the area, the small town was called Villa de Santa María de Los Lagos. The town soon became a shelter for travelers and an outpost for the Spanish caravans as they traveled the silver route from the rich mines of Zacatecas to Mexico City.

By March of 1574, the menace of Indian attack caused so many people to flee that only eight residents of Lagos stayed on. By the end of the century, however, the Chichimeca War had ended, and the growth of Santa María de los Lagos resumed. With the end of the hostilities, my indigenous ancestors evolved from nomadic belligerents into sedentary agriculturalists who then went to work for their former adversaries, the Spaniards.

---

[6] Philip Wayne Powell, *op. cit.* p. 69.

INDIAN ANCESTORS OF COLONIAL LAGOS

Spain instituted a racial order called the casta system through which Mexico's population came to be legally distinguished based on race. This system was used to deny and prescribe legal rights to individuals and to assign them social prestige. In particular, distinguishing the population on the basis of parental origin became an adequate legal method of according economic privilege and social prestige to Spaniards. [1]

The Founding of a Family

The story of the Morales family begins with Miguel Morales and María de la Cruz, my great-great-great-great-great-great-grandparents. Miguel and María's first child, Lorenza Morales, was baptized on June 26, 1684 at the Immaculate Conception (*Inmaculada Concepción*) Church in Ciénega de Mata, which lies almost directly north of Lagos.

With the baptism of their next daughter, Michaela, on November 6, 1690, Miguel and María started bringing their children to the Church of the Assumption at Santa María de los Lagos for baptism. Another daughter, Juana, was baptized on August 17, 1692.

---

[1] Martha Menchaca, *op. cit.*, p. 62.

On the following page, we have reproduced the baptism record for my great-great-great-great-great-grandfather, Juan Miguel Morales, who was born six years later. In part, the Spanish translation of this very brief document states that on June 24th, 1698, the parish priest Father Guerra solemnly baptized and poured holy oil on Juan, an Indian, the legitimate son of Miguel de Morales and María de la Cruz. The document also gives the names of the *padrinos* (godparents). Three years later, on October 4, 1701, Miguel and María baptized their last child, Miguel, at Santa María.

On February 15, 1722, Juan Morales, the twenty-three year old son of Miguel and María, was married to Paula Petrona de la Cruz. Paula Petrona was only sixteen at the time of her marriage. Her baptism in Lagos had taken place on July 19, 1705, when Father Jacinto González de Lario duly recorded that he had baptized and poured holy oil and chrism on Paula Petrona, a newly born Indian girl who was the legitimate daughter of Martten de los Reyes and Silveria de Ortega.

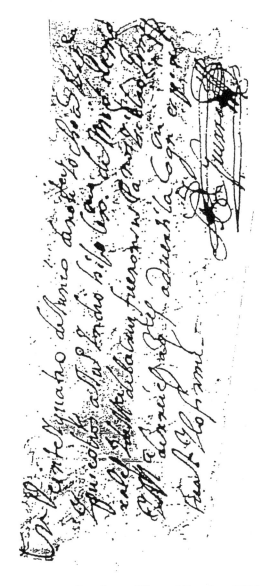

Baptism of Juan Morales, 1698

INDIAN ANCESTORS OF COLONIAL LAGOS

It is worth noting that surnames such as de la Cruz and de los Reyes were frequently given to Indian peasants by their parish priests (especially in Lagos). In most parts of Mexico, indigenous people – after being Christianized and Hispanicized – assumed Christian given names and Spanish surnames. This was considered a necessary part of their indoctrination into the new religion and a rejection of the old pagan religions they formerly adhered to. If one had chosen to keep his indigenous name, it would have been construed as an attempt to retain his former culture and religion.

And so it was that Juan Morales and Paul Petrona – both classified as Indians in all the available records – commenced their marriage as subjects of the Spanish King Felipe V and as parishioners of Santa María de los Lagos Church. The union of Juan Morales and Paula Petrona would produce at least six children born in the years following their marriage: María (February 9, 1723), Francisco (March 1, 1725), Antonia Bernarda (March 17, 1727), Joséph Joachin (April 3, 1729), Antonio Simon (May 6, 1731), and Dionicia María Anna (April 19, 1733).

INDIAN ANCESTORS OF COLONIAL LAGOS

My direct ancestor was their second child, Francisco, whose baptism took place in the Lagos Church on March 1, 1725. In the margin of Francisco's baptism document, Father Francisco Reynoso inscribed "Francisco Mazelo yndio de San Xavier," which means that the baptized child was Francisco Marcelo Morales, an Indian from San Xavier.

In this document – which we have chosen not to reproduce here – Father Reynoso states that he baptized solemnly Francisco Marselo, an Indian (*yndio*) child who was eight days old and the legitimate son of Juan de Morales and Paula Petrona, residents of the Hacienda of San Xavier. The *padrino* (godfather) was listed as Xavier Gonzalez, a resident of Quarenta.

The Racial Classifications of My Ancestors

Twenty-nine years later, Francisco Morales would be married under the name "Francisco Xavier Morales." It appears that my ancestor Francisco Morales dropped his middle name (Marselo) and adopted the middle name of Xavier, possibly from his godfather and birthplace. Francisco Morales grew up in the vicinity of Lagos and met a young girl classified by the parish records as a "mulata."

A mulata (the female gender) or a mulato (the male gender), by definition, is a person who has one white parent and one parent of African descent. However, the criteria that parish priests used for determining the racial classification of parishioners was not cut in stone and varied from one individual to another.

Professor Robert H. Jackson, the author of *Race, Caste, and Status: Indians in Colonial Spanish America*, has written about the "imprecision" of the Catholic priests in classifying their mixed-raced parishioners. He explains that "race categories assigned to *castas* [persons of mixed racial origin] were based on the assumption that priests or colonial officials could classify the ancestry, or more accurately the bloodlines, of an individual on the basis of skin color."[2]

---

[2] Robert H. Jackson, *Race, Caste, and Status: Indians in Colonial Spanish America* (Albuquerque, New Mexico: University of New Mexico Press, 1999), p. 4.

"However," Professor Jackson comments, "other criteria also figured in the creation of racial identity such as stereotypical assumptions about culture, behavior, and, in the case of rural populations, the place of residence and the form of land tenure or usage." And, Professor Jackson concludes, this "identity creation occurred in a variety of documents including parish registers, censuses, and tribute records.[3]

Thus we can see that the classification of mulato or mulata may well have been a judgment call on the part of one parish priest. And this judgment was frequently based on the parishioner's skin color. Thus, it might be possible for one parishioner to carry two or more racial classifications in his life.

On November 4, 1754, the parish priest at Santa María de los Lagos recorded the marriage of Francisco. This document – which we have not reproduced here – has been translated from Spanish into English as follows:

---

[3] *Ibid.*

INDIAN ANCESTORS OF COLONIAL LAGOS

In the Parish of Lagos on the Fourth of November in 1754, having read the three marriage banns, as required by the Holy Council of Trent, on three holy days in Holy Mass, and having found no impediment to marriage resulting, I, Father Miguel Antonio de Gurruehaga asked for the consent of FRANCISCO XAVIER MORALES, Indian, originally from and a resident of this parish, legitimate son of Juan Morales and Paula de Thorres; and LUCRECIA DE MONTELONGO, free mulata, originally from and a resident of San Cristobal, legitimate daughter of Thoribio de Montelongo and María Ana Gomes, and having announced both, married them by these words (marriage vows)....

Montelongo is a beautiful Spanish surname which may have originated in three villages of Spain: Arzúa, La Coruña and San Ciprián. "Longo" is the archaic Spanish word for "luengo" which means "long." Therefore, we may infer that Montelongo may be a reference to a "long mountain."[4]

---

[4] Richard D. Woods and Grace Alvarez-Altman, *Spanish Surnames in the Southwestern United States: A Dictionary* (Boston: G. K. Hall & Co. 1978), p. 93.

However, the ethnic origins of my Montelongo ancestors from Lagos is shrouded in uncertainty. The Montelongo branch of my family started with Lucrecia de Montelongo's grandparents, Pedro Montelongo and Pasquala de Espiritu Santo – both classified as mulatos. On January 16, 1692, the parish priest in Lagos recorded the following marriage of Pedro and Pasquala. Although we are not reproducing this document here, we will present our English translation of the Spanish document:

> *On the 16th of January 1692, I married and blessed within the church, PEDRO MONTELONGO, a free mulato, resident of this villa, parents names not known, with PASQUALA DE ESPIRITU SANTO, a free mulata, resident of this parish, in the Hacienda de San Cristobal, legitimate daughter of Lasaro de Torres and Margarita de Rivera...*

Pedro and Pasquala had at least five children who were born between 1696 and 1707, including Torribio Montelongo, who was baptized by Father Jacinto González de Lario in Lagos church on April 22, 1699.

INDIAN ANCESTORS OF COLONIAL LAGOS

It is important to note that the spelling of both given names and surnames in colonial Mexico is highly inconsistent. Two parish priests who may have been born, raised and educated in different parts of Spain would have recognized different spellings for the same name. Thus, we can see that Torribio Montelongo's first name was also spelled as Thoribio (in his daughter's marriage record). Such variant spellings of certain words are extremely common.

Like his parents before him, Torribio Montelongo – the father of Lucretia – was classified as a mulato. More than thirty years after his birth, Toribio Montelongo – now identified as Torribio Efigenio Montelongo – would be married to Maríana Gomes.

The marriage document of Torribio and Maríana, recorded in the Parish Church of Lagos is reproduced on the following pages and has been translated, in part, as follows:

> *In the Parish of the Village of Lagos on the 20th of February, 1730, having read the three marriage banns as arranged (required) by the Holy Council of Trent on three holy days in*

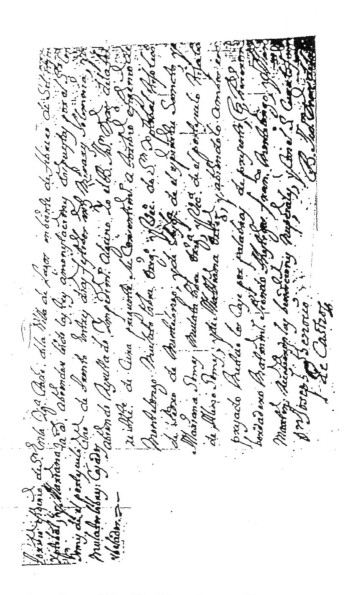

Marriage of Torribio Montelongo, 1730

> *Holy Mass, and having found no impediments to marriage resulting, I Father Juan Diaz de la Torre, deputy priest, asked for the consent of TORIBIO EFIGENIO DE MONTELONGO, free mulato, originally from and a resident of San Cristobal, legitimate son of Pedro de Montelongo and of Pasquala de el Espiritu Sancto, and MARÍANA GOMES, free mulata, originally from and resident of El Portyuelo, legitimate daughter of Alexo Gomes and Mathiana Ortiz, both having expressed mutual consent, I married them by the present words (marriage vows).....*

Five years later, Maríana gave birth to their daughter Lucrecia Rosalia Montelongo, my great-great-great-great-grandmother. Lucrecia was born in the Hacienda of San Cristobal (where many of my ancestors appear to have lived) and baptized sixteen days later in the Lagos church on May 9, 1735. She too was classified as a mulata libre (free mulata).

My great-great-great-grandfather, José Nosiforo Morales, the son of Francisco Xavier Morales and Lucrecia Montelongo, was baptized in Lagos on August 10, 1755. This ancestor, like his parents and grandparents before him, was classified

INDIAN ANCESTORS OF COLONIAL LAGOS

as a person of mixed origin. It is important to realize that during the colonial era, many persons of African descent lived and worked alongside the Indians of colonial Lagos. In the following chapter we will discuss the influence and status of the African in colonial Lagos society.

SLAVERY IN COLONIAL MEXICO

The African slaves... possessed some degree of internal social differentiation. Taken as a group, the social divisions among the slaves were not as clearly marked as those existing within the other two groups. The realities of slavery were not conducive to the emergence, development, and maintenance of a well-defined social structure among the slave population. Slaves were not like free people; their status as human chattels defined and limited their individual potential and subjected them to the will and caprice of the master. [1]

African Ancestors in Lagos

During the middle of the Eighteenth Century, some of my Morales ancestors were classified not as Indians or mestizos, but as mulatos, which implies at least a partial African ancestry.

Most people are not very aware of the presence of African slaves in colonial Mexico. But it helps for us to remember that the Spaniards brought slaves to every corner of their American empire. One of the most detailed works about slavery in Mexico is the noted historian Colin A. Palmer's *Slaves of the White God: Blacks in Mexico, 1570-1650.*

---

[1] Colin A. Palmer, *Slaves of the White god: Blacks in Mexico, 1570-1650* (Cambridge, Massachusetts: Harvard University Press, 1976), p. 37.

SLAVERY IN COLONIAL MEXICO

"The introduction of African slaves into Mexico," explains Dr. Palmer, "was in part a response to the labor shortage stemming from the decline of the indigenous population during the sixteenth century. Spanish mistreatment of the Indians and a number of disastrous epidemics contributed to this demographic catastrophe."

As we explained in Chapter 3, the native peoples of the Americas had no immunity to a wide range of "Old World" diseases, especially smallpox, measles and the typhus-like sickness called matlazáhuatl. Terrible epidemics struck Mexico in 1520, 1548, 1576-1579 and 1595-1596, killing millions of indigenous peoples. As a result, the population of Mexico – estimated at 25 million inhabitants in 1519 – dropped to 1,375,000 by 1595 and to 1,075,000 by 1605.[2]

As the indigenous population of Mexico declined, the colonial economy became more complex. The first silver

---

[2] Woodrow Borah and Sherburne Cook, *The Aboriginal Population of Central Mexico on the Eve of the Spanish Conquest*, Ibero-Americana, No. 45 (Berkeley and Los Angeles, 1963), p. 4

mines were opened as early as 1534 and the cultivation of sugar cane started to take root in Mexico around the same time. Soon textile workshops, cattle ranches and haciendas would be established.

"All of these enterprises," notes Dr. Palmer, "required an adequate and dependable labor force for their sustenance. For the Spanish proprietors involved, an unpaid servile labor force was the most desirable." Faced with labor-intensive businesses and a demographic vacuum, the Spanish authorities convinced themselves that the importation of African slaves in large numbers was their only solution.[3]

In 1542, King Carlos V promulgated the New Laws of the Indies, essentially abolishing slavery in Mexico and the rest of the Americas. This event gave Spanish businessmen a stronger impetus to bring more Africans to the shores of North America.

---

[3] Colin A. Palmer, *op. cit.*, pp. 2-3.

SLAVERY IN COLONIAL MEXICO

Dr. Palmer explains that "As a group, African slaves performed the most strenuous tasks on the plantation. The belief that, as workers, Africans were superior to Indians was shared by the Spaniards in New Spain and in the other colonies". In the Sixteenth Century, many Spaniards held the popular belief that one Black slave could equal the labor output of four Indians.[4]

In the period from 1521 to 1594, government estimates indicate that 36,500 slaves were brought to Mexican shores. Then, from 1595 to 1622, 322 slaving ships delivered 50,525 slaves to Mexican ports. These slaves represented almost half of the total number of slaves brought to the Spanish West Indies. For the period 1622 to 1639, another 23,500 slaves were brought to Mexico. With these figures in mind, one can say that a total of 110,525 slaves were legally shipped to Mexico from 1521 to 1639.[5]

---

[4] Gonzalo Aguirre Beltrán, *La Población Negra de México, 1519-1810* (Mexico, 1972: 2nd edition).

[5] *Ibid.*, pp. 15-16, 28; Archivo General de Indias, Contratación, 5758, 5766, sección Segunda, 2894. and Indiferente General, 2766.

SLAVERY IN COLONIAL MEXICO

In the early decades of the slave trade, many of the slaves came from Guinea-Bissau and Sene-gambia. According to Dr. Palmer, slaves from this area "enjoyed a favorable reputation in the Indies for their alleged docility and trustworthiness." The ethnic groups taken from Senegambia included the Tukulor, the Wolof, and the Malinke. The Kassanga, the Bram, the Banyun and the Biafada were taken from the coastal areas of Guinea-Bissau. From the coast of Sierra Leone came the Landuma, the Baga, and the Temne peoples. The Bakongo peoples were brought in from Central and southern Africa.[6]

In the Seventeenth Century, the majority of the slaves brought to Mexican shores came principally from Angola and the Congo. In a study of 402 African-born slaves during the Seventeenth Century, Aguirre Beltrán found that 75.4 percent came from Central Africa, specifically from Luanda in Angola. Mr. Beltrán also notes that 20.9 percent of the

---

[6] Colin A. Palmer, *op. cit.*, p. 20.

slaves came from West Africa. Many of the latter group were Wolof people from Senegal.[7]

Dr. Palmer explains that "it is possible to establish the ethnic origin of some of the Mexican slaves by consulting the bills of sale, which were required to carry information regarding the ethnic origin, age, and sex of the slaves old." However, slaves who were smuggled into Mexico illegally to avoid paying taxes were not tallied in this manner.[8]

Dr. Palmer has estimated that the total number of African-born slaves brought to Mexico from the earliest years of the Sixteenth Century to the day that the institution was abolished (1827) numbered about 200,000.[9] It is believed that the African and Black population of Mexico never reached more than two percent of the total population. The majority of slaves brought to the shores of Mexico were

---

[7] *Ibid.*, pp. 22-23; Gonzalo Aguirre Beltrán, *op. cit.*, p. 241.

[8] Colin A. Palmer, *op. cit.*, pp. 20-22.

[9] *Ibid.*, p. 3.

male. With a lack of female Africans, most of these men eventually chose Indian or mestizo women as spouses.

The *Siete Partidas* laws granted slaves the right to select their spouses. Slave masters were thus forbidden from intervening in this decision.[10] Professor Menchaca observes that "this legislation was of monumental importance because it became the gateway for the children of slaves to gain their freedom. Due to the lobbying efforts of the Catholic Church the children of Black male slaves and Indian women were declared free and given the right to live with their mother."[11]

With laws that granted freedom to the children of a slave who married into other racial classifications, it is very obvious to see the motivation of this class to seek outside partners. And, it is likely that some of my mulato ancestors in Lagos were able to do exactly this.

---

[10] Martha Menchaca, *op. cit.*, p. 63.

[11] *Ibid.*, pp. 61-62.

RACE IN COLONIAL MEXICO

Within fifty years of the conquest, Spanish-Indian relations were redefined and race became a principal factor in the social and economic organization of Spanish colonial society.[1]

The Caste System in Mexico

Nearly all of my ancestors who lived in the vicinity of Lagos de Moreno during the Seventeenth Century and Eighteenth Century were mulatos, mestizos or indios. A mestizo was defined as a person that was half-Indian and half-Spanish. Like mulatto, mestizo may not have been used accurately and it is possible that a mestizo may have had African blood too.

Several works have discussed the use of racial classification in Spanish colonial Mexico. One of the best works to consult is Professor Martha Menchaca's very informative *Recovering History, Reconstructing Race: The Indian, Black, and White Roots of Mexican Americans.*

While the Spaniards and Europeans living in Mexico "enjoyed the highest social prestige and were accorded the

---

[1] Martha Menchaca, *op. cit.*, p. 49.

most extensive legal and economic privileges," my Indian, mestizo and mulato ancestors brought up the other end of the social spectrum.

"The social and economic mobility of the rest of the population," writes Professor Menchaca, "was seriously limited by the legal statuses ascribed to their ancestral groups." As a matter of fact, Professor Menchaca continues, "Indians were accorded little social prestige in Mexican society and were legally confined to subservient social and economic roles regulated by the Spanish elite. Most Indians were forced to live in a perpetual state of tutelage controlled by the church, state, or Spanish landowners."[2]

Professor Menchaca notes that "Indians were economically more privileged than mestizos because they held title to large parcels of communal land protected by the crown and the Catholic Church" through the *corregimiento* system.[3]

---

[2] *Ibid.*, p. 63.

[3] *Ibid*, pp. 63-64; Clarence H. Harring, *The Spanish Empire in America* (New York: Harbinger, 1963); Magnus Mörner, *Race Mixture in the History of Latin America* (Boston: Little, Brown and Company, 1967).

RACE IN COLONIAL MEXICO

On the other hand, my mestizo and mulato ancestors did not have land reserved for their use, as my indigenous ancestors most likely did. In fact, mestizos were, according to Professor Menchaca, "barred by royal decree from obtaining high and mid-level positions in the royal and ecclesiastical governments." Additionally, they were prohibited from becoming priests in central Mexico.[4]

Worse still was the social classification of *afromestizos* – persons of mixed Indian, African and Caucasian blood. "Because they were of partially African descent," states Professor Menchaca, "...they were stigmatized and considered socially inferior to Indians and mestizos... afromestizos were subjected to racist laws designed to distinguish them from mestizos and to impose financial and social penalties upon them."[5]

When my great-great-great-grandfather, José Nosiforo Morales, was married to his first wife on February 25, 1783 in Lagos, he was classified as a free mulato. José's bride,

---

[4] Martha Menchaca, *op. cit.*, pp. 63-64.

María Tereza Aranda, was classified as a mestiza. The marriage record that the parish priest created for this special event described José Nosiforo Morales as a free mulato from the Hacienda of Magueyes and as the legitimate son of Francisco Morales and Lucrecia Montelongo. His wife, María Tereza Aranda, a mestiza from Quarenta, was the legitimate daughter of José Antonio Aranda and María Feliciana Guzman.

The Delgado Family

María Tereza eventually died and eleven years later, with several small children in his care, José Morales was remarried on February 8, 1794 to my great-great-great-grandmother, María Josefa Delgado.

In the marriage document of the Lagos church, José was classified as an Indian, not a mulato. Once again, the varying perceptions of parish priests led to a second racial classification for my ancestor. José's new bride, María Josefa Delgado, was described by the parish register as a sixteen-year-old Indian girl from the Sabinda Hacienda, and

---

[5] Martha Menchaca, *op. cit.*, p. 64.

the legitimate daughter of José Dionicio Delgado (deceased) and María Quiteria Delgado.

My ancestor María Josefa was also descended from a long line of Indian and mulato inhabitants from the vicinity of Lagos. My ancestry through María Josefa extends back to the middle of the Seventeenth Century, when most of the family members were laborers for Nicholas Muños. The Descendancy Chart on the following page starts with Luis de Campos and María de la Cruz (the great-great-great-grandparents of María Josefa Delgado) and ends with my generation.

Although we are not going to explore this branch of the family in great detail, we have decided to present several family documents in order to make a point about the imprecision and ambiguity of racial classifications employed in the parish records of colonial Mexico.

1. Luis de Campos
 sp: Maria de la Cruz
 └ 2. Juana de Campos
  sp: Juan Delgado (m.1680)
  └ 3. Juan Delgado (b.1694-Lagos de Moreno)
   sp: Felipa de Vega (m.1716)
   └ 4. Jose Leonicio Delgado (b.1723-Lagos de Moreno)
    sp: Josefa Ramirez Torres (b.1722-Lagos de Moreno;m.1745)
    └ 5. Jose Dionisio Delgado
     sp: Rita Quiteria de Lara (m.1773)
     └ 6. Maria Josefa Delgado (b.1776-Lagos de Moreno)
      sp: Jose Nosiforo Morales (b.1755-Lagos de Moreno;m.1794)
      └ 7. Jose Casimiro Morales (b.1804-Moreno de los Lagos)
       sp: Zeferina Valades (b.1818-Ojuelos,Jalisco;m.1836)
       └ 8. Austacio Morales (b.1845-Aguascalientes)
        sp: Juana Salas (b.1849-Aguascalientes;m.1873)
        └ 9. Olayo Morales (b.1875-Aguascalientes)
         sp: Juana Luevano (b.1885-Villa Hidalgo,Jalisco;m.1903;d.1951)
         └ 10. Daniel Morales (b.1914-Houston,Texas)
          sp: Pabla Bessie Dominguez (b.1915-Canadian,Texas;m.1937)
          └ 11. Donna Morales (b.1947-Kansas City,KS)
           sp: David Stewart

Descendancy Chart of Campos and Delgado Ancestors

RACE IN COLONIAL MEXICO

On the following page, we have presented a document, dated February 15, 1744. This is the marriage record of Carlos Antonio and María de la Encarnación Valades, the maternal grandparents of Maria Josefa Delgado. This document is translated into English as follows:

In the Parish of Lagos on the 15th of February of 1744, having read the three marriage banns as required by the Holy Council of Trent on three holy days in Solemn Mass, and no impediments to marriage having resulted, I, Father Francisco Xavier Solis ask for the consent of CARLOS ANTONIO, a free mulato, originally from and a resident of this parish in Quarenta, legitimate son of Geronimo Disiderio, and of Nicolasa Dimas, and MARÍA DE LA ENCARNACION VALADES, a free mulata, originally from and a resident of the above-mentioned parish in Sabinda, legitimate daughter of Alonso Valades and of Josefa de la Pena, and both having expressed mutual (consent), I married and veiled them by the words of the present (marriage vows), that are true marriage, the witnesses present: Joachin Cervantes and Julia Padilla. They received the blessed nuptials, and with him, the priest, I signed it.
Francisco Xavier Solis

Marriage Record of Carlos Antonio, 1744

Now, we will move on one more generation down the line. On the following page, we have reproduced the 1777 marriage record for my great-great-great-great-grandparents, Jose Dionicio Delgado, an Indian, and Rita Quiteria de Lara, also an Indian. Their marriage took place in Lagos de Moreno and our translation of that document is as follows: [6]

> *In the Parish of Lagos on the 10th of July 1773, having read the marriage banns in solemn Mass on three holy days, on the 13th, 20th, and 24th of June, as required by the Holy Council of Trent, I, Father Miguel Días asked for the consent of JOSE DIONICIO DELGADO, an Indian, originally from and a resident of this parish in the post of Quarenta, legitimate son of Leon Delgado and Josefa Ramires, and RITA QUITERIA DE LARA, an Indian, originally from and a resident of this parish in Sabinda, legitimate daughter of Carlos Antonio de Lara, and of María Valades, and having expressed mutual consent, I married them by the present words (marriage vows)....*
> *Jose Reyes Gomes de Aguilar*
> *Miguel Diaz Sandiz*

---

[6] The marriages of 1773 for Lagos de Moreno, Jalisco are contained on Microfilm 0221516 (Salt Lake City: Genealogical Society of Utah, 1958).

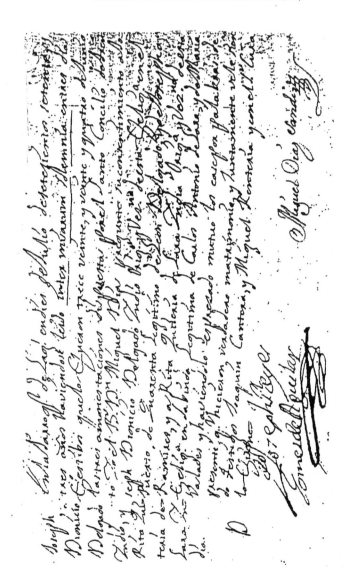

Marriage of José Dionicio Delgado, 1773

RACE IN COLONIAL MEXICO

The Rita Quiteria de Lara who was married in 1777 is the daughter of Carlos Antonio and María de la Encarnación de Valades, whose marriage record was presented on page 132. The significance of this document is that the parish priest has classified the parents of the Indian girl, Rita Quiteria de Lara, as mulatos. The ambiguity in racial terms used by parish priests thus may have been the result of varying perceptions by different priests with varying educational and cultural backgrounds.

I am not certain how many children José Morales and María Josefa Delgado had, but I do know that their son, José Casimiro Morales, who was baptized at the age of 10 days on March 12, 1804 in Lagos, is my great-great-grandfather. Casimiro, like both of his parents, was classified as an Indian in the church baptism record, which we have chosen not to reproduce here.

The Mexico that José Casimiro Morales grew up in was a rapidly changing country. It was this ancestor who would move from Lagos de Moreno to Aguascalientes and a new life.

AN EMPIRE DISINTEGRATES

The war of independence had disastrous effects on the national economy. During the war, fields were destroyed and agricultural production declined, leaving the country in a crisis. There was insufficient food to feed the masses. In the mining industry production practically came to a halt, as many workers had left the mines to join the war and machinery had been damaged. This produced a financial strain, because the mining industry had been one of Mexico's strongest assets, generating employment for a large segment of the population... [1]

Reform and Discontent

The next twenty years would mark an important turn of events for the Mexican people. In addition to her Caribbean, Central American, and Mexican possessions, Spain had gained possession of France's extensive Louisiana territory in 1769. However, in 1800, Emperor Napoleon of France forced Spain to return Louisiana to France by the Treaty of San Ildefonso. Three years later, France sold Louisiana to the United States.

The loss of Louisiana was the beginning of the end for Spain's large American empire. The stage for the political revolutions about to take place was set by an important

---

[1] Martha Menchaca, *op. cit.*, p. 162.

AN EMPIRE DISINTEGRATES

development that took place in Europe early in the Nineteenth Century. In 1807, Emperor Napoleon lured King Carlos IV of Spain and his family to France for a visit. Once there, the Spanish royal family was thrown into prison, and King Carlos was forced to abdicate the throne.

After forcing out King Carlos, Napoleon announced that his brother, Joseph Bonaparte, would become the new King of Spain. Soon after, in March 1808, 100,000 French troops invaded Spain under the pretense of protecting the country's coastline from the British, with whom France was in a state of war.

Emperor Napoleon I quickly defeated the Spanish and entered Madrid in triumph. But the Spanish people, true to their tradition of defiance toward invaders, resisted the French occupation bitterly and carried on an effective guerrilla warfare against the uninvited invaders. In spite of the 300,000 French troops standing on Spanish soil, the guerrilla tactics of the Spanish people never left the conquerors secure in their position.

AN EMPIRE DISINTEGRATES

By 1813, the Spanish people, with the help of British forces, were able to drive the French from the Iberian Peninsula. In the following year, King Ferdinand VII, the son of King Carlos IV, was restored to his throne.

However, the rumblings of discontent in Mexico had become more visible in recent decades. By 1810, out of a total population of at least six million people, 3,676,281 were Indian, while another 1,328,707 were classified as castas (mestizos, mulatos and afromestizos) of various racial mixtures. Together, these racial groups constituted 84 percent of Mexico's population.[2]

During "the absence of Spain's legitimate monarch," observes Professor Menchaca, the Cortés (Spain's parliament) "was composed of liberal thinkers, including representatives from Mexico, who passed legislation reforming the autocratic government into a constitutional monarchy." These reforms were directed at both Indians and mestizos in the hope of making them "loyal subjects by

---

[2] *Ibid.*, pp. 157-158; Gonzalo Aguirre Beltrán, *op cit.*

accelerating the Indians' assimilation and opening economic opportunities for both peoples."[3]

"To implement these desired objectives," Professor Menchaca comments, "the Cortés abolished the 'racial caste system" and gave Indians, mestizos, and free afromestizos many of the legal rights of Whites." Then, on September 25, 1810, Indians in Mexico were released from their centuries-old obligation of paying tribute to the crown and local government authorities. Henceforth, they would be taxed in the same manner as other subjects of the Empire.[4]

A few months later, on February 9, 1811, the Royal Crown decreed that Indians were permitted to raise any crop they wanted. They were also given the right to enter any profession and to transact business with whomever they

---

[3] Martha Menchaca, *op. cit.*, pp. 157-158; Thomas D. Hall and David J. Weber, *Mexican Liberals and the Pueblo Indians, 1821-1829*, New Mexico Historical Review, 59 (1): 5-32.

[4] Martha Menchaca, *op. cit.*, p. 158; Woodrow Borah, *Justice by Insurance: The General Indian Court of Colonial Mexico and the Legal Aides of the Half-Real* (Berkeley: University of California Press, 1983), p. 395.

chose. "In sum," Professor Menchaca concludes, "all economic and occupational restrictions were lifted."[5]

The Struggle for Independence.

But, by this time, revolution was inevitable and the first shots of the Mexico's War of Independence had already been heard throughout the land. Early on the morning of September 16, 1810, Father Miguel Hidalgo y Costilla (1753-1811) summoned the largely Indian and mestizo congregation of his small Dolores parish church in Guanajuato and urged them to take up arms and fight for Mexico's independence from Spain. His *Grito de Dolores (Cry of Dolores)* maintained the equality of all races and called for redistribution of land.

Within days, a motley band of poorly armed Indians and mestizos made their way to San Miguel, enlisting hundreds of recruits along the way. San Miguel fell to the rebel forces, but when Hidalgo's forces reached the city of

---

[5] *Ibid.*, p. 396; Martha Menchaca, *op. cit.*, p. 158; Cecil Alan Hutchinson, *Frontier Settlement in Mexican California: The Hijar-Padres Colony and Its Origins, 1769-1835* (New Haven, Conn: Yale University Press, 1969), p. 10.

AN EMPIRE DISINTEGRATES

Guanajuato on September 28, they met with stiff resistance from royalist forces. Before the day was over, a fierce battle had cost the lives of 500 Spaniards and 2,200 Indians. But the rebels had captured the city and in October, they moved on to take Zacatecas, San Luis Potosí, and Valladolid.

By October, Hidalgo, with a revolutionary army now numbering 80,000 men, approached Mexico City. Although his army defeated a small, well-equipped Spanish army outside of the city, Hidalgo – whose forces were short on ammunition – ordered a northward retreat.

From this point, the Spanish forces began a campaign to recapture lost territory. A few months later, in March 1811, Hidalgo and other rebel leaders were captured in Coahuila. Most of the rebel leaders were executed as traitors. Found guilty of heresy and treason, Father Hidalgo was executed on July 31st.

The revolutionary cause was next taken up by Father José María Morelos y Pavón (1765-1815). By the Spring of 1813, Morelos' rebel army had encircled Mexico City and isolated the capital from both coasts. However, within six months, the Spanish military was able to break the siege and recapture lost territory once again. In the Fall of 1815, Morelos was captured and executed by a firing squad. With his execution, the Independence movement reached its nadir.

Over the next five years, some sporadic guerilla warfare continued to plague the Spanish military. However, the Mexican Independence movement would receive unexpected help from a foreign ally. In 1820, a revolt of the Spanish military in Spain brought about a renewed vitality on the part of the Mexican people. In December of 1820, a royalist officer, Agustín de Iturbide (1783-1824), switched allegiance and made common cause with the rebel movement.

On February 24, 1821, Agustín de Iturbide declared the Plan of Iguala, calling for an independent, constitutional monarchy headed by an emperor. He entered Mexico City on September 27, 1821, and took power soon after. The treaty of Córdoba' was signed by Agustín de Iturbide and the last Viceroy, Juan O'Donojú, on August 24, 1821. This treaty recognized Mexico's independence. However, on May 19,

AN EMPIRE DISINTEGRATES

1822, the Congress named Iturbide as the constitutional emperor of Mexico. Mexico now moved from an absolute monarchy to a constitutional monarch.

CITIZENS OF A MEXICAN REPUBLIC

After independence Mexico experienced a half-century of transition. The country was much changed, especially in the realm of politics and governance, but the core of everyday life retained its essential characteristics. Neither thousands of years of indigenous tradition and culture, nor 300 years of Spanish colonial heritage disappeared. Most Mexicans ate the same foods, resided in the same kind of dwellings, and wore the same kinds of clothes as had their ancestors for decades if not centuries.[1]

After independence the government suspended the collection of statistical racial enumerations in government documents on the grounds that this practice had been used to distinguish the races and hence used for discriminatory purposes. Allegedly such records were no longer necessary because most people, with the exception of slaves, had been declared citizens with equal rights and obligations..[2]

The Republic of Mexico

It soon became apparent that Iturbide did not have the support he needed to remain Emperor of Mexico. On December 1, 1822, the commander of the Veracruz garrison, Antonio López de Santa Anna Pérez de Lebrón (1794-1876), leading a force of 400 troops, rose in rebellion against

---

[1] Mark Wasserman, *Everyday Life and Politics in Nineteenth Century Mexico: Men, Women, and War* (Albuquerque: The University of New Mexico Press, 2000), p. 22.

[2] *Ibid.*, p. 166.

Iturbide. On that day, Santa Anna proclaimed a republic. On February 1, 1823, José Antonio Echáverri, the Captain General of Veracruz, joined forces with Santa Anna. Within two weeks, Itrubide abdicated his throne and fled into exile. Mexico had finally become a true Republic without a monarch.

The early years of independence were difficult years for Mexico. The War of Independence and the subsequent separation from Spain, according to the historian Mark Wasserman, had taken "an enormous toll politically, psychologically, and financially." The colonial economy was "devastated" and "mining, its fulcrum, was in ruins." But the worst was yet to come, and "a long series of foreign invasions and civil wars followed, consuming immeasurable human and material resources."[3]

War, Insurrection, and Instability

In 1829, the Mexican army defeated an attempt by Spain to reconquer Mexico. At about the same time, Mexico was

---

[3] *Ibid.*, p. 6.

forced to deal with an insurrection by the American inhabitants of Texas. In 1836, Texas won its independence. Two years later, a French invasion of Mexico was defeated.

But the most disastrous war of all was the War of 1846-1848 with the United States. By the end of this war, Mexico had lost almost half of her territory to the United States. In the meantime, the Caste (Race) War erupted in the Yucatán (1847). From 1857-1860, a devastating civil war (The War of the Reform) polarized the entire country. This war was followed by a French invasion and occupation that lasted from 1861 to 1867.[4]

In the decades following her independence, Mexico's political situation seemed to be in a constant state of turmoil. Between 1824 and 1857, Mexico had 16 presidents and 33 provisional chief executives, for a total of 49 national administrations. In 1829, the office of President changed hands three times, and in 1833, the same office changed

---

[4] *Ibid.*

hands seven times. In 1844, 1846, 1855, the office would change hands four times in each of those years.[5]

During this period, the military dominated the highest echelons of the federal government. From 1821 to 1851, only six civilians served as President, while a total of 15 generals also held the office. Three of the civilian presidents lasted mere days in office. Anastasio Bustamante (1780-1853) held the position of President for the longest consecutive period of time (four and a half years), while General Santa Anna served as chief executive a total of eleven times.[6]

During these perilous years of instability, writes Professor Wasserman, "the core of everyday life retained its essential characteristics." Many Mexican citizens lived in the countryside on *haciendas* (large land-holdings). Most haciendas employed both permanent inhabitants and temporary laborers. The permanent employees included

---

[5] *Ibid.*, p. 46; Donald Fithian Stevens, *Origins of Instability in Early Republican Mexico* (Durham, Duke University, 1991), p. 11.

[6] Mark Wasserman, *op. cit.*, p. 46.

resident peons, tenants, or sharecroppers, while temporary laborers would be brought in from neighboring villages. Many villagers relied on the estates for work that would supplement their meager earnings from working their own lands. However, the hacienda system in Mexico was severely weakened starting in 1821 because of shrinking markets for their products and uncertain political conditions.[7]

Casimiro Morales

Sometime around 1830, my great-great-grandfather, Casimiro Morales, probably about 26 years of age, left Santa María de los Lagos (which, by this time, had been renamed Lagos de Moreno after the revolutionary patriot, Pedro Moreno). He moved to Palo Alto along the present-day boundary of Jalisco and Aguascalientes. However, he probably worked at one of the sixteen haciendas located in and about the small town of Cienega de Mata.

---

[7] Mark Wasserman, *op. cit.*, pp. 22-29. Professor Wasserman discusses the haciendas, villages, and the mining camps in depth on pages 22 through 34 of this work.

CITIZENS OF A MEXICAN REPUBLIC

On June 16, 1823, Jalisco, formerly the Intendancy of Guadalajara, had become a state within the new Republic. According to the historian Stanley C. Green, Jalisco "emerged from the revolutionary era with imperialistic ambitions, prepared to challenge the city of Mexico for leadership. Its population in 1826 was reckoned at 656,830, second only to the state of Mexico."[8]

However, Aguascalientes, the new home of Casimiro Morales, still belonged to the state of Zacatecas. Located in the center of Mexico between the states of Jalisco and Zacatecas, the modern state of Aguascalientes has a total area of 5,589 square kilometers and a population of at least 850,000. Although Aguascalientes occupies a mere 0.3% of the national territory of the Mexican Republic, it holds a strategic location within Mexico and sits along an important link between Mexico City in the south and Ciudad Juárez in the north.

---

[8] Stanley C. Green, *The Mexican Republic: The First Decade, 1823-1832* (Pittsburgh: The University of Pittsburgh Press, 1987), p. 19.

Aguascalientes was detached from Zacatecas and granted the status of territory on May 23, 1835, after the state forces of Zacatecas were defeated by General Santa Ana's federal forces during an unsuccessful attempt to assert their autonomy.

Two decades later, a Federal Decree of November 10, 1853 granted Aguascalientes the status of Department. And finally, on October 29, 1857, the Federal Government bestowed the title of the "Free and Sovereign State of Aguascalientes," thus giving it full statehood rights.

In 1836, Casimiro Morales was married to 18-year-old Zeferina Valades in the church of Cienega de Rincon (in Jalisco). Because Casimiro's marriage record is hard to read, we have not reproduced this document here. However, the English translation of this marriage document is as follows:

In the church of Cienega de Rincon, auxiliary of the Parish of Ojuelos, on the 26th of June, in the year 1836, having presided over the marriage banns, and having read the marriage banns as required by the Holy Council of Trent on three holy days in solemn mass, on the 5th, 12th, and ....of June, and having found no impediments to marriage resulting, I, Father Roman Lopéz, with license from the parish, assisted... united in marriage CASIMIRO MORALES, single, 30 years old, originally from the Sabinda Hacienda in Lagos, and resident of this place for six years in Palo Alto, legitimate son of José Nosiphoro Morales, deceased, and of San José Delgado, and ZEFERINA VALDADES, a celibate girl, 18 years of age, originally from Palo Alto, and the legitimate daughter of Vicente Valadez, deceased, and of Rufina Campos....

Over the next twenty years, Casimiro Morales and his wife Zeferina Valades would have several children, some of whom were baptized in Cienega de Mata. However, in the 1840s, the family moved to Rancho del Muerto (Ranch of the Dead) in Aguascalientes, where they became laborers and continued to have children. In 1846, Casimiro and Zeferina had a son named, Austacio (also spelled Eustacio). After Austacio's birth, two more daughters were born and baptized in Aguascalientes: Maria Benigna Morales (February 20, 1853) and Lorenza Morales (September 8, 1855).

Casimiro and Zeferina continued to raise their family on the Rancho del Muerto well into the 1860s. Then, on June 1, 1863, their son Austacio Morales was married to one Juana Salas, also a native of the Rancho del Muerto. This marriage of my paternal great-grandparents took place at La Parroquia de la Asunción de Nuestra Señora (The Parish of the Assumption of Our Lady) in the capital city of Aguascalientes. The document recorded in the parish records has been translated as follows:

In the Parish of Aguascalientes on the First of June of 1863, Father Don Juan Avila, with license from the Parish, after having proceeded with the necessary information and the marriage bans in preparation, and no impediments to marriage having resulted, I married and blessed within the church AUSTACIO MORALES, single, 18 years of age, originally from and a resident of Rancho del Muerto, legitimate son of Casimiro Morales and Zeferina Valadés, who are living, with JUANA SALAS, celibate, 14 years of age, originally from and a resident of the same Rancho, legitimate daughter of Gregorio Salas and Lucia Torres, who are living....

CITIZENS OF A MEXICAN REPUBLIC

During the 1870s, the Morales family moved to the Hacienda of Santa María, outside of Aguascalientes. Here, they worked as laborers and raised a small family. Austacio Morales and Juana Salas had several children, including my paternal grandfather, Olayo (Eulalio) Morales, who was born in 1875.

Olayo and Juana Luevano Morales.

After the turn of the century, my grandfather met a young girl named Juana Luevano. Juana's ancestors had been among the earliest Spanish settlers of Aguascalientes, some of them arriving in 1593 from Spain. It is through Juana that I inherit my Spanish blood. Juana was born in Villa Hidalgo, which is located in the state of Jalisco just south of the boundary between Jalisco and Aguascalientes.

Today, Villa Hidalgo has a population of 20,000 and occupies fourth place in the manufacture of textile products in Mexico. In earlier centuries, it was sometimes called Paso de Carretas (Cart's Crossing), in reference to its reputation as a stopover for carts traveling to and from Aguascalientes.

CITIZENS OF A MEXICAN REPUBLIC

I do not know the circumstances under which my grandparents, Olayo and Juana, met, but it is possible that both of their families were employed at the same Rancho. When they were married on January 18, 1903, the civil wedding took place in Cieneguilla, a small town in Aguascalientes just a few miles northeast of Villa Hidalgo. At the time of this marriage, Olayo was a 22-year-old day laborer living and working in Cieneguilla. However, my grandfather, it was noted in the civil records of this marriage, had been born in the Hacienda of Santa María. Juana Luevano was 16 years old and the legitimate daughter of Tiburcio Luevano and Manuela Martinez.

Olayo and Juana settled down to married life in the Hacienda de la Cantera in Aguascalientes. The first child born to the union of Olayo and Juana was my Uncle Carmen, who was born in 1905 in Aguascalientes. Their second child, Celestino, was born on April 8, 1908. By this time, negative forces in the Mexican Republic were setting the groundwork for what would soon develop into a bloody civil war that would affect the lives of every Mexican citizen.

A NATION ON THE BRINK

Porfirio Díaz was president of Mexico for thirty-one of the thirty-five years between 1876 and 1911. He ruled over an era of unprecedented peace, political stability, and... economic growth. There were neither foreign wars, nor widespread civil conflicts. Díaz built his regime with a shrewd combination of consensus and repression... However, as revealed by the economic and political crises that occurred between 1907 and 1910, it was a dictatorship built on quicksand. When challenged by a multi-class opposition coalition and armed insurrection in 1910, the Díaz regime collapsed.[1]

The Mexican Revolution

As Olayo and Juana raised their small family in early years of the Twentieth Century, Mexico started to experience profound social and political changes. The era of Mexican politics that lasted from 1876 to 1910 is usually referred to as *The Porfiriato*, for Porfirio Díaz, who served as President through six terms of office starting in 1876. During this period, according to Mr. Meyer, "Mexico entered a period of sustained economic growth the likes of which she had never before experienced."[2]

---

[1] Mark Wasserman, *op. cit.* p. 209.

[2] Michael C. Meyer and William L. Sherman, *op. cit.*, p. 439.

However, writes Mr. Meyer, the peace, prosperity, and stability of this era was preserved in part by the use of "brute force." Through "adroit political maneuvering, threats, intimidation, and, whenever necessary, callous use of the federal army," Porfirio Díaz maintained himself in power.

In spite of the modernization of Mexico's industry and the prosperity of the small upper class, Mexico remained an "overwhelmingly rural country... dominated by the hacienda complex." And, unfortunately for the average Mexican citizen, "the abuses of the system were exacerbated markedly during the Díaz regime."[3]

By 1894, one-fifth of the total land mass of Mexico was owned by land companies "and some 134 million acres of the best land had passed into the hands of a few hundred fantastically wealthy families." According to the Mexican census of 1910, 8,245 haciendas existed in the Republic and half of all rural Mexicans lived and worked on them. Mr. Meyer writes that these millions of laborers "were worse off

---

[3] *Ibid.*, pp. 453-458.

financially than their rural ancestors a century before" and "in terms of purchasing power correlated with the price of corn or cheap cloth," the Mexican peón was actually twelve times poorer than the average American farm laborer.[4]

By 1910, President Díaz had come under sharp criticism from his political opponents for the autocratic nature of his rule. It was only a matter of time before a social revolution would become necessary. The opposition eventually coalesced around an eccentric northern landowner, Francisco I. Madero (1873-1913). On November 20, 1910, Madero, who had taken refuge in the United States, issued a call for an armed uprising. By May of the next year, President Díaz was forced to resign and flee the country.

However, the resignation of Díaz did not bring stability to Mexico. Instead, the turmoil became more intense, especially after the overthrow and assassination of Madero in February 1913. General Victoriano Huerta, a general who was born in a small Jalisco village, assumed the office of

---

[4] *Ibid.,* pp. 460-461.

A NATION ON THE BRINK

President after having overthrown Madero. But Huerta's stay in office came to an end on July 8, 1914, when he was forced to resign. "The years following Victoriano Huerta's ouster," according to Mr. Meyer, "are the most chaotic in Mexican revolutionary history as the quarrels among erstwhile allies began."[5]

Some have estimated that the lost of life in the Mexican Revolution (1910-1920) was between 1.5 and 2 million. "In a country with a population of roughly 15 million in 1910," writes Mr. Meyer, "few families did not directly feel the pain as one in every eight Mexicans was killed. Even Mexico's high birthrate could not offset the casualties of war. The census takers in 1920 counted almost a million fewer Mexicans than they had found only a decade before."[6]

With this major loss of life, the already fragile Mexican economy was nearly destroyed. Jobs were scarce in many parts of the country, and the average daily wage of the

---

[5] *Ibid.*, p. 535.

[6] *Ibid.*, p. 552.

common farm laborer in Mexico did not exceed twenty-five cents a day. Railway laborers in Mexico were making fifty to seventy-five cents a day in 1910. By comparison, railway workers in the United States made $1.25 a day.[7]

The displacement and turmoil caused by the Mexican Revolution led to the emigration of as many as a million Mexicans in the years between 1910 and 1920. My family – with its roots in Mexico stretching back countless centuries – joined this mass movement in search of a new life in the United States.

[7] Arthur F. Corwin, ed., *Immigrants – and Immigrants: Perspectives on Mexican Labor Migration to the United States*, Contributions in Economics and Economic History, No. 17 (Westport, Connecticut: Greenwood Press, 1978), pp. 41, 88.

AN AMERICAN EXPERIENCE

Mexican emigration to the United States was essentially an economic phenomenon; there was a demand for inexpensive labor in one country and an unlimited number of unemployed laborers in another. Mexico's unemployment rate, coupled with the political disorders, religious disturbances, poverty, and revolutionary unrest, provided plenty of incentive for hundreds of Mexican men to travel northward to find a better life.[1]

We are all citizens of one world; we are all of one blood. To hate a man because he was born in another country, because he speaks a different language, or because he takes a different view on this subject or that, is a great folly. Desist, I implore you, for we are all equally human. Let us have but one end in view, the welfare of humanity.[2]

Crossing the Border

After the Revolution began, many Mexican families began to move northward in the hopes of avoiding hostilities. During these dangerous times, my grandparents, Olayo Morales and Juana Luevano, decided to leave the chaos and conflict of Mexico for a new life in the United States.

---

[1] Cynthia Mines, *Riding the Rails to Kansas: The Mexican* Immigrants (1980, not published), p. 22.

[2] Quote by John Comenius (1592-1670) from an article in the Holy Bible of Daniel S. Morales, Sunday school teacher.

It is possible that they may have crossed the border more than once in the years between 1908 and 1912. The alien registration record made for my grandmother Juana Luevano Morales is reproduced on the following page. According to this document, Juana had stated that she crossed the border for the first time on February 20, 1906. We have not been able to locate relevant border-crossing records to confirm this or other crossings before 1912.

As a matter of fact, Juana's alien registration record states that she crossed the border on March 15, 1912. However, the actual border crossing document – which we have not reproduced here – states that Juana and Olayo actually crossed the border on November 19,1912, carrying with them their two small children, Carmen and Celestino. The Immigration Service (then a section of the Department of Commerce and Labor) made a separate manifest of each family member as they crossed the border on that day at Eagle Pass, Texas.

AN AMERICAN EXPERIENCE

6872610

Form AR-2
OFFICE USE

UNITED STATES DEPARTMENT OF JUSTICE
IMMIGRATION AND NATURALIZATION SERVICE

ALIEN REGISTRATION FORM

1. ☆(a) My name is _____ **Juana** (none) **Luevano vda. de. Morales**
   (FIRST NAME) (MIDDLE NAME) (FAMILY NAME)

   ☆(b) I entered the United States under the name of _____ **Juana L. Morales**

   ☆(c) I have also been known by the following names _____ **Juana Luevano (maiden name)**
   (include maiden name if a married woman,
   professional names, nicknames, and aliases):

2. ☆(a) I live at _____ **1028 S. 22nd St., Kansas City, Wyandotte, Kansas**
   (STREET ADDRESS OR RURAL ROUTE) (CITY) (COUNTY) (STATE)

   ☆(b) My post-office address is _____ **Same as above**
   (POST OFFICE) (STATE)

3. ☆(a) I was born on _____ **Unknown Unknown 1888**
   (MONTH) (DAY) (YEAR)

   ☆(b) I was born in (or near) _____ **Villa Hidalgo, Jalisco, Mexico**
   (CITY) (PROVINCE) (COUNTRY)

4. ☆ I am a citizen or subject of _____ **Mexico**
   (COUNTRY)

5. ☆(a) I am a (check one):   ☆(b) My marital status is (check one):
   Male☐¹ Female☒²   Single☐¹ Married☐² Widowed☒³ Divorced☐⁴
   ☆(c) My race is (check one): White☒¹ Negro☐² Japanese☐³ Chinese☐⁴ Other _____

6.   I am **5** feet **0** inches in height, weigh **112** pounds, have **Grey** hair and **Brown** eyes
   (COLOR) (COLOR)

7. ☆(a) I last arrived in the United States at _____ **Eagle Pass, Texas** on _____ **March 15, 1912**
   (PORT OR PLACE OF ENTRY) (MONTH, DAY, AND YEAR)

   ☆(b) I came in by _____ **on foot across the bridge.**
   (NAME OF VESSEL, STEAMSHIP COMPANY, OR OTHER MEANS OF TRANSPORTATION)

   ☆(c) I came as a (check one): Passenger☐¹ Crew member☐² Stowaway☐³ Other **Pedestrian**
   ☆(d) I entered the United States as a (check one): Permanent resident☒¹ Visitor☐² Student☐³
   Treaty merchant☐⁴ Seaman☐⁵ Official of a foreign government☐⁶ Employee of a
   foreign government official☐⁷ Other

   ☆(e) I first arrived in the United States on _____ **February 20, 1906**
   (MONTH) (DAY) (YEAR)

8. ☆(a) I have lived in the United States a total of _____ **42**

   ☆(b) I expect to remain in the United States _____ **permanently.**
   (PERMANENTLY, OR DURATION OF EXPECTED STAY)

9.   (a) My usual occupation is _____ **Housewife** (b) My present occupation is _____ **Housewife**

   ☆(c) My employer (or registering parent or guardian) is _____ **None**
   (NAME)

   whose address is _____
   (STREET ADDRESS OR RURAL ROUTE) (CITY) (STATE)

   and whose business is _____

   All items must be answered by persons 14 years of age, or older. For children under 14 years of age, only the items marked with
   a star (☆) must be answered by the parent or guardian. All answers must be accurate and complete.

Alien Registration for Juana Luevano Morales

AN AMERICAN EXPERIENCE

Olayo and Juana had arrived at the border by traveling along the *Ferrocarrilles Nacionales de Mexico* (Mexican National Railway), which terminated at Piedras Negras, located across the Rio Grande from Eagle Pass. As Juana moved across the border, she was described as being in good health. Both she and Olayo stated that their destination was Houston in Lamar County, Texas.

Although many Mexican migrants found employment with the railroads, the historian Arnold de León, in his work *Ethnicity in the Sunbelt: Mexican Americans in Houston*, explained that "opportunities opened up in occupations generated by the oil-related industries lured more Mexicans to the city, especially after the completion of the Ship Channel in 1914."[3]

Like many other Mexicans, my family found a place to live in the Second Ward, which was the recipient of most Mexican newcomers. Just before Olayo had arrived with his

---

[3] Arnoldo de León, *Ethnicity in the Sunbelt: Mexican Americans in Houston* (College Station: Center for Mexican American Studies, University of Houston, 2001), p. 10.

family, a new church, Our Lady of Guadalupe Church, had been built to accommodate the Mexican populace. The first Mass was celebrated in the new church on August 18, 1912.[4]

Daniel Morales

My father, Daniel Morales, was born in Houston on September 23, 1914. On October 21, 1914, Olayo and Juana took Daniel to Our Lady of Guadalupe Church and had him baptized. One of his godparents was his maternal uncle, Jose Luevano.

Six years later, according to the 1920 Federal census, Olayo Morales, a native of Mexico, lived at 304 Walker Street in Houston, Harris County, Texas. Living in Enumeration District 66, Olayo was listed as a 30-year-old white male who had immigrated in 1911. His occupation was listed as "driver" of an "express wagon."

Olayo's wife, Juana, was also listed as 30 years old, even though she was actually 35 years of age. The children listed

---

[4] Sister Mary Paul Valdez, *The History of the Missionary Catechists of Divine Providence* (not published, 1978), pp. 2-4.

were Carmen (son, 15 years old), Celestino (son, 13 years old), Maria (daughter, 7 years old), and Daniel (son, 5 years old). Maria and Daniel were both born in the United States, while all the other members of the family were natives of Mexico.

Shortly after 1920, the Morales family decided to go north. In Scotts Bluff County, Nebraska, there was a great need for laborers to help with the sugar beet harvest. Recruiters in the Houston area enlisted the services of Olayo and his entire family. Originally, the work was seasonal, but after Olayo died and Juan remarried, the family decided to stay in Kiowa Township.

When the census-taker arrived at their doorstep in 1930, the Morales family had undergone very profound changes. The head of the household was Louis Garcia, the stepfather of Daniel and Juana's second husband. My grandmother, Juana, was listed as "Jenny Garcia," and my father's given name was spelled "Danial."

AN AMERICAN EXPERIENCE

Daniel was fifteen years old at this time and described his occupation as "laborer" on a "beat farm." Daniel's 5-year-old stepsister, Carmen Garcia, also lived in the household. On the following page we have reproduced a picture of a very young Daniel Morales wearing his sombrero, which helped shield him from the sun when he labored in the Nebraska sugar beet fields as a teenager and young man.

In 1932, Daniel Samuel Morales – as he was called for most of his life – came to Kansas. He first worked for the railroad and was married to one Agripina Llanos. However, that marriage ended very soon when Agripina died in childbirth. Soon after he met Bessie Dominguez, a native of Texas and the daughter of Zacatecas immigrants.

Bessie (Pabla) Dominguez was a beautiful woman with very exotic Indian features, an inheritance of her ancestors who spent many centuries working the mines in northern Zacatecas. The Dominguez family had arrived in Kansas in 1917 as one of the earliest Mexican families in the Kansas City area.

AN AMERICAN EXPERIENCE

Daniel Morales, circa 1935

AN AMERICAN EXPERIENCE

On April 18, 1937, after a short courtship, Daniel and Bessie were married in Jackson County, Missouri. Over the years, Daniel and Bessie would have a total of eight daughters: Jenny, Olivia, Mary Ellen, Eleanor, Ruth, Carol, Donna, and Abigail. I was the sixth daughter out of the eight children.

Life In Kansas

Daniel and Bessie were both very attractive people. On the following page, we have reproduced a picture of them taken sometime around 1943, when they stood up as "best man" and "maid of honor" at the wedding of a friend. Life in Kansas City, however, was difficult for most Mexican Americans during the 1930s and 1940s.

During the 1920s and 1930s, the state of Kansas – with its extensive railroad yards and meatpacking industry – became a major destination for Mexican immigrants and American-born Mexican-Americans from other states. By 1930, in fact, the Mexican and Mexican-American population of Kansas represented the seventh largest Mexican ancestral

Daniel and Bessie Morales, 1943

group in the U.S. They also comprised the second largest immigrant population in the state after the Germans.[5]

However, in spite of their increasing numbers, the author Cynthia Mines tells us that the "Mexican settlers were set apart linguistically, economically, religiously, and culturally from the mostly white, Protestant, middle class Kansans with which they were surrounded. They tended to stay within their colonies, some eventually building their own schools and churches, and ventured out only to buy necessities."[6] Mexican Americans – like their Native American brothers of the United States – were looked down upon by some elements of American society.

Mexicans, according to Ms. Mines, "had a higher ethnic visibility, because of their darker skin complexion, and they were not as easily assimilated into society as were the

---

[5] Robert Oppenheimer, "Acculturation or Assimilation: Mexican Immigrants in Kansas, 1900 to World War II," *The Western Historical Quarterly*, Vol. XVI, No. 1 (January 1985), p. 431.

[6] Cynthia Mines, *Riding the Rails to Kansas: The Mexican Immigrants* (1980, not published), p. 22.

Germans, the largest immigrant group to Kansas."[7] Professor Robert Oppenheimer of the University of Kansas has written a great deal about the segregation of and discrimination against Mexican Americans in Kansas:[8]

> Overt racial bias was common. Throughout Kansas, Mexicans remained segregated, and Anglos viewed Mexicans with suspicion even when they left the confines of the barrios for the day.... Until the 1950s, in virtually every Kansas town and city, Mexicans and Mexican-Americans remained segregated in movie theaters and were often restricted from some sections of city parks, churches, and other public facilities. Windows of some businesses contained signs stating "No Mexicans allowed," and Mexicans could not obtain haircuts in local barbershops.

Not long after my parents were married, my father took a job as a laborer for the Santa Fe Railroad. The Santa Fe was a major employer of Mexican Americans in Kansas City, and many members of my mother's family had been working for

---

[7] *Ibid.*, p. 6.

[8] Robert Oppenheimer, *op. cit.*, pp. 431-432.

them for a long time. In these early years, my parents lived in a small place at 1015 South 24th Street. As the Great Depression gripped our nation during the late 1930s, my father struggled to make a living and feed a small family at the same time.

When World War II began with the attack on Pearl Harbor in December 1941, my father decided that he must serve his country and enlist in the Army. However, my mother was adamantly opposed to such a move. With two daughters and a wife to feed, Daniel had too many responsibilities and, in the end, he decided not to enlist.

My father, however, did find a way to contribute to America's war effort. Soon after the war had begun, Daniel Morales started a new job at the Kansas City Structural Steel Company and moved his small family to 820 South 6th Street. My father's employer fabricated much of the steel for the buildings that were constructed in the Kansas City area. However, when World War II started, many private industries were asked to contribute to the common war effort. As a result, Kansas City Structural Steel Company was given the responsibility of building 407 landing craft barges for the United States Navy.[9]

World War II was a great struggle against tyranny and every American family had to make sacrifices. When my mother's brother, Erminio Dominguez, was captured by the Germans in 1944, my father offered his shoulder for my mother to lean on. When my Uncle Louis Dominguez was killed in action while fighting the Germans on March 31, 1945, once again my father was the pillar of strength that my mother and her family came to rely upon for solace and moral support.

To make ends meet for his growing family, my father had to take on several jobs. After the war, he became a clerk for the C.R.I.&P Railroad (Rock Island Railroad) and, at the same time, worked at the Muelbach Hotel in Kansas City as a waiter. But, in addition to these jobs, Father also took a great interest in theology. Because he was a religious man,

---

[9]   Source: "Kansas   City   War   Contribution,"   Online: <http://www.geocities.com/kcghostsquadron/CAF-KC-History.html>. November 27, 2002. Copyright 1996-2002 Commemorative Air Force, Inc.

AN AMERICAN EXPERIENCE

he decided to become a Sunday school teacher at the First Mexican American Baptist Church in Kansas City.

My father was an energetic and compassionate man. Because he felt that it was important to put into action his religious principles, he practiced charity both at home and in the outside world. For two decades, Daniel Morales would go down to the railroad yards to find the Mexican laborers who had ridden the rails into Kansas City looking for work. He would take these poor illiterate strangers who had little or no knowledge of the English language and bring them to the Salvation Army store. Here, he would buy them shoes and shirts to wear.

After clothing them, Father would bring the men home where my mother would cook them a nice meal. He would give them a place to stay in our house while he went out to find jobs for them. To my father, this service was his way of practicing his Christian charity.

Service to God and God's children meant a great deal to Father. Although he had no sons, he became a Scout Master for Boy Scout Troop #230 and continued in that capacity for 17 years. Taking part in the spiritual growth of others was so meaningful and important to Daniel that he continued to teach Sunday school for over forty years.

My father worked his three jobs for many years. His energy and enthusiasm for life and service endured for most of his life. In 1975, he retired from his job at the Rock Island Railroad. In the 1990s, he became increasingly frail with stomach problems. He was diagnosed with stomach cancer and passed away on November 16, 1996 at Trinity Lutheran Manor. His funeral was held on Tuesday, November 19 at Simmons Funeral Home, followed by burial at Maple Hill Cemetery. At the time of his death, my father left behind his wife, eight children, 16 grandchildren and 16 great-grandchildren.

Reflections on the Passage of Time

My ancestors lived in Aguascalientes and Jalisco for many centuries. But the vast majority of ethnic groups existing in these two states during the pre-Hispanic era ceased to exist as distinguishable cultural entities during the Sixteenth and

AN AMERICAN EXPERIENCE

Seventeenth Centuries. Little is known of their religions or languages and most of the customs they practiced are long forgotten to the rest of the world.

Not forgotten, however, is the long struggle that they waged against the Spaniards and Indians who intruded upon their native lands. Not forgotten are the religion and the language that they learned from Spanish padres and administrators. Not forgotten is the fact that these Native American people are alive and living in me and millions of other Mexican Americans.

Family history – like human history – is a process of evolution: cultural, spiritual, linguistic, genetic, and personal. From Chichimec warrior to Indian peasant, from pagan to Christian, from Indian to Mexican, from mestizo to ciudadano, from hacienda laborer to railroad employee, from student to teacher, and from Mexican to Mexican American, we have forged a new path from one generation to the next – but always in North America.

BIBLIOGRAPHY

Adams, Richard E.W. *Prehistoric Mesoamerica*. Boston: Little, Brown and Company, Inc., 1977.

Aguirre Beltrán, Gonzalo. *La Población Negra de México, 1519-1810*. Mexico City: Ediciones Fuente Cultural.

Altman, Ida and Lockhart, James. *Provinces of Early Mexico: Variants of Spanish American Regional Evolution*. Los Angeles: UCLA Latin American Center Publications, University of California, Los Angeles, 1976.

Anna, Timothy E. *Forging Mexico, 1821-1835*. Lincoln, Nebraska: University of Nebraska Press, 1998.

Bakewell, P. J. *Silver Mining and Society in Colonial Mexico: Zacatecas, 1546-1700*. Cambridge: Cambridge University Press, 1971.

Bancroft, Hubert Howe. *History of Mexico: Volume III. 1600-1803*. San Francisco: A. L. Bancroft & Company, Publishers, 1883.

Borah, Woodrow. *Justice by Insurance: The General Indian Court of Colonial Mexico and the Legal Aides of the Half-Real*. Berkeley: University of California Press, 1983.

Chávez, John R. *The Lost Land: The Chicano Image of the Southwest*. Albuquerque: University of New Mexico Press, 1984.

Cheetham, Sir Nicolas. *Mexico: A Short History*. New York: Thomas Y. Crowell Company, 1970.

BIBLIOGRAPHY

Cockcroft, James D. *Mexico: Class Formation, Capital Accumulation, and the State.* New York: Monthly Review Press, 1983.

Commemorative Air Force, Inc. "Kansas City War Contribution," Online: <http://www.geocities.com/kcghostsquadron/CAF-KC-History.html>. November 27, 2002. Copyright 1996-2002.

Corwin, Arthur F. "Mexican Emigration History, 1900-1970: Literature and Research," *Latin American Research Review,* VIII (Summer 1973), 3-24.

Davies, Nigel. *The Aztecs: A History.* Norman, Oklahoma: University of Oklahoma, 1980.

Davies, Nigel. *The Ancient Kingdoms of Mexico.* London: Penguin Books, 1990.

De León, Arnoldo de León. *Ethnicity in the Sunbelt: Mexican Americans in Houston.* College Station: Center for Mexican American Studies, University of Houston, 2001.

Dobyns, Henry F. "Estimating Aboriginal American Population," *Current Anthropology 7* (1966), pp. 395-449.

Dunne, Peter Masten. *Pioneer Jesuits in Northern Mexico.* Berkeley: University of California Press, 1944.

Ewing, Russell C. et al. *Six Faces of Mexico.* Tucson, Arizona: The University of Arizona Press, 1966.

BIBLIOGRAPHY

Funk & Wagnalls Corporation. *The World Almanac and Book of Facts, 1995*. Mahwah, New Jersey: Funk & Wagnalls Corporation, 1994.

Gamio, Manuel. *Mexican Immigration to the United States*. Chicago: The University of Chicago Press, 1930.

Garcia, Juan R. *Mexicans in the Midwest, 1900-1932*. Tucson, Arizona: The University of Arizona Press, 1996.

Gerhard, Peter. *The Northern Frontier of New Spain*. Princeton, New Jersey: Princeton University Press, 1982.

Green, Stanley C. *The Mexican Republic: The First Decade, 1823-1832*. Pittsburgh: The University of Pittsburgh Press, 1987.

Grimes, Barbara F. (ed.). "Languages of Mexico" Online: http://www.ethnologue.com/show_country.asp?name=Mexico (November 10, 2002) from *Ethnologue: Languages of the World* (14th edition), Dallas, Texas: SIL International, 2001.

Hall, Thomas D. and Weber, David J. *Mexican Liberals and the Pueblo Indians, 1821-1829*, New Mexico Historical Review, 59 (1): 5-32.

Hanks, Patrick and Hodges, Flavia. *A Dictionary of Surnames*. Oxford: Oxford University Press, 1988.

BIBLIOGRAPHY

Instituto Nacional de Estadística Geografía e Informática (INEGI). *Estados Unidos Mexicanos. XII Censo General de Población y Vivienda, 2000. Tabulados Básicos y por Entidad Federativa. Bases de Datos y Tabulados de la Muestra Censal.* Mexico City, 2001.

Instituto Nacional de Estadística Geografía e Informática (INEGI), "Social and Demographic Statistics," Online: http://www.inegi.gob.mx/difusion/ingles/fiest.html. November 11, 2002.

Jackson, Robert H. *Race, Caste, and Status: Indians in Colonial Spanish America.* Albuquerque, New Mexico: University of New Mexico Press, 1999.

Jennings, Francis. *The Founders of America: How Indians Discovered The Land, Pioneered in it, and Created Great Classical Civilizations, How They Were Plunged Into a Dark Age by Invasion and Conquest, and How They Are Reviving.* New York: W. W. Norton & Company, Inc., 1993.

Jiménez, Carlos M. *The Mexican American Heritage.* Berkeley, California: TQS Publications, 1994 (2nd edition).

Lombardi, Cathryn L. et al. *Latin American History: A Teaching Atlas.* Madison, Wisconsin: University of Wisconsin, 1983.

Marks, Richard Lee. *Cortés: The Great Adventurer and the Fate of Aztec Mexico.* New York: Alfred A. Knopf, 1994.

BIBLIOGRAPHY

Mason, J. Alden. "The Native Languages of Middle America" in *The Maya and Their Neighbors.* New York: Appleton-Century Company, 1940..

Mecham, J. Lloyd. *Francisco de Ibarra and Neuva Vizcaya.* Durham, North Carolina, Duke University Press, 1927.

Meier, Matt S. and Rivera, Feliciano. *The Chicanos: A History of Mexican Americans.* New York: Hill and Wang, 1972.

Meier, Matt S. and Rivera, Feliciano. *Mexican Americans, American Mexicans: From Conquistadors to Chicanos.* New York: Hill and Wang, 1993.

Menchaca, Martha. *Reconstructing History, Constructing Race: The Indian, Black, and White Roots of Mexican Americans.* Austin: University of Texas Press, 2001.

Meyer, Michael C. and Sherman, William L. *The Course of Mexican History.* New York: Oxford University Press, 1987.

Millon, Rene. "Social Relations in Ancient Teotihuacan" in Eric Wolf, ed., *The Valley of Mexico: Studies in Pre-Hispanic Ecology and Society* (Albuquerque: University of New Mexico Press, 1976), 205-248.

Millon, René. "Teotihuacán: City, State and Civilization," in *Archaeology*, edited by Jeremy A. Sabloff and with the assistance of Patricia A. Andrews, *Supplement to the Handbook of Middle American Indians, Vol.1*, Austin, Texas: University of Texas Press, 1981.

Mines, Cynthia. *Riding the Rails to Kansas: The Mexican Immigrants*. Kansas, 1980.

Morales, Donna S. and Schmal, John P. *My Family Through Time: The Story of a Mexican-American Family*. 2000, Los Angeles, California (not published).

Morales, Donna S. and Schmal, John P. *Mexican-American Genealogical Research: Following the Paper Trail to Mexico*. Bowie, Maryland: Heritage Books, 2002.

Moreno González, Afredo. *Santa Maria de Los Lagos*. Lagos de Moreno: D.R.H. Ayuntamiento de Los Lagos de Moreno, 1999.

Mörner, Magnus. *Race Mixture in the History of Latin America*. Boston: Little, Brown and Company, 1967.

Oppenheimer, Robert. "Acculturation or Assimilation: Mexican Immigrants in Kansas, 1900 to World War II," *The Western Historical Quarterly*, Vol. XVI, No. 1 (January 1985).

Powell, Philip Wayne. *Soldiers, Indians and Silver: North America's First Frontier War*. Tempe, Arizona: Center for Latin American Studies, Arizona State University, 1973.

BIBLIOGRAPHY

Ramírez Flores, José. *Lenguas Indígenas de Jalisco*, of "Colección: Historia: Serie: Documentos e Invetigación No. 1," Guadalajara, Jalisco: Gobierno del Estado de Jalisco, Secretaria General de Gobierno, 1980.

Rutter, Larry G. *Mexican Americans in Kansas: A Survey and Social Mobility Study, 1900-1970*. Master's Thesis, Kansas State University, 1972.

Schmal, John P. *The Morales-Dominguez Family History*. Los Angeles, California, 2000.

Simpson, Lesley Byrd. *Many Mexicos.* Berkeley, California: University of California Press, 1971.

Smith, Michael E. *The Aztecs.* Cambridge, Massachusetts: Blackwell Publishers, Inc., 1996.

Spicer, Edward. "Ways of Life" in Russell C. Ewing et al., *Six Faces of Mexico.* The University of Arizona Press, 1966.

Sugiyama, Saburo. "Archaeology of Teotihuacan, Mexico," Online: http://archaeology.la.asu.edu/teo/intro/intrteo.htm. August 20, 2001. Copyright 1996, Project Temple of Quetzalcoatl, Instituto Nacional de Antropología e Historia, Mexico/ Arizona State University Department of Anthropology.

Valdez, Sister Mary Paul. *The History of the Missionary Catechists of Divine Providence* (not published, 1978).

BIBLIOGRAPHY

Van Young, Eric. "The Indigenous Peoples of Western Mexico from the Spanish Invasion to the Present: The Center-West as Cultural Region and Natural Environment," in Richard E. W. Adams and Murdo J. MacLeod, *The Cambridge History of the Native Peoples of the Americas, Volume II: Mesoamerica, Part 2.* Cambridge, U.K.: Cambridge University Press, 2000, pp. 136-186.

Waldman, Carl. *Atlas of the North American Indian.* New York: Facts on File Publications, Inc., 1985.

Waldman, Carl. *Encyclopedia of Native American Tribes.* New York: Facts on File Publications, 1988.

Wasserman, Mark. *Everyday Life and Politics in Nineteenth Century Mexico: Men, Women, and War.* Albuquerque: The University of New Mexico Press, 2000.

Weigand, Phil C., "Considerations on the Archaeology and Ethnohistory of the Mexicaneros, Tequales, Coras, Huicholes, and Caxcanes of Nayarit, Jalisco, and Zacatecas," in William J. Folan (ed.), *Contributions to the Archaeology and Ethnohistory of Greater Mesoamerica.* Carbondale, Illinois: Southern Illinois University Press, 1985.

Williamson, Edwin. *The Penquin History of Latin America.* New York: Penguin Books, 1992.

Woods, Richard D. and Alvarez-Altman, Grace. *Spanish Surnames in the Southwestern United States: A Dictionary.* Boston, Massachusetts: G. K. Hall & Co., 1978.

INDEX

BIOGRAPHIES

Donna S. Morales.

Donna Morales is a native of Kansas City. Ms. Morales and Mr. Schmal have known each other for 12 years and collaborated on an unpublished book chronicling the 400-year history of Ms. Morales' family. Ms. Morales is a family research historian and is a member of the Society for Hispanic Historical and Ancestral Research (SHHAR) and Familia. She occasionally contributes article to the SHHAR newsletter, www.somosprimos.com. Ms. Morales works for an insurance company in Houston, Texas.

John P. Schmal.

John Schmal is a native of Hermosa Beach, California. He is a genealogist, with a specialty in Mexican lineages. Mr. Schmal belongs to the Association of Professional Genealogists, Familia, the Genealogy Society of Hispanic America, and the Society for Hispanic Historical and Ancestral Research (SHHAR). Mr. Schmal is the Staff Historian and Indexer for the SHHAR newsletter, www.somosprimos.com, and gives professional lectures on Mexican-American genealogy and indigenous Mexico. Mr. Schmal works for a publishing company in Chatsworth, California.